THE
MAKING OF AMERICA
SERIES

COLUMBIA

HISTORY OF A SOUTHERN CAPITAL

By 1893, the streetcar was electrified and Sylvan Brothers had moved into the bank building on the northeast corner of Main and Hampton Streets. Bicycles had also gained popularity by this time and were quick and reliable transportation around town.

THE
MAKING OF AMERICA
SERIES

COLUMBIA
HISTORY OF A SOUTHERN CAPITAL

LYNN SIMS SALSI
WITH MARGARET SIMS

ARCADIA
PUBLISHING

Published by Arcadia Publishing
Charleston, South Carolina

Printed in the United States of America

Library of Congress Catalog Card Number: 2002114943

For all general information contact Arcadia Publishing at:
Telephone 843-853-2070
Fax 843-853-0044
E-Mail sales@arcadiapublishing.com
For customer service and orders:
Toll-Free 1-888-313-2665

Visit us on the Internet at www.arcadiapublishing.com

DEDICATION:

FOR: BURKE SALSI—FRANK SIMS, JR.
JAY SWYGERT—BO SALSI—BRIAN SALSI

Front cover: *By 1890, there were five volunteer fire companies and twenty-two police officers. The city police and volunteer firemen are gathered for review in front of the State House. c. 1895.*

CONTENTS

ACKNOWLEDGMENTS

Burke, Bo, Brian Salsi for photographs, research, and for exploring historical sites.
Jay and Maria Swygert and Wayne Smalldridge for their encouragement.
Janet Metcalfe for her assistance with graphics and for locating photographs, Wilbur Smith Associates in Columbia for use of photographs, Frances Sloan Fulmer of Aiken for use of photographs and for her interest in this project.
A very special thanks to Mr. and Mrs. Talbot Bissell of Greensboro, North Carolina. Mr. Bissell is the great, great, great grandson of Colonel Thomas Taylor. He is also the grandson of Henry Taylor Williams who served in the Confederacy. Mrs. Bissell is the granddaughter of Gustavus Augustus Follin, assistant adjutant general who served with States Rights Gist. He was among the last to leave Columbia before the Union troops entered. The Bissells made available photographs, books, their private collection of original Civil War letters, and related family tales of their ancestors.
Lester Bates, Jr. for sharing memories, facts, and photos of his father; Katherine Keyes for sharing the family album and oral history about her great, great, great, great grandfather, Reverend Henry Mood; Thanks for the memories: Woody Windham, John Wrisley, Bill Benton, Miriam Ford.
Reverend Mark Alexander, Washington Street Methodist Church; United Daughters of the Confederacy, especially Ellen Bissell.
The Richland County Public Library, the Columbia Art Museum, the Robert Mills House, the Hampton Preston House, Columbia Preservation Society, the South Caroliniana Library, the McKissick Library, the South Carolina Department of Archives, the South Carolina Museum.
The South Carolina Historical Society in Charleston; The Confederate Relic Room, William J. Long, Registrar; Thanks to Joe Rogers, Director of the South Carolina Department of General Services; Clemson University; The Southern Collection—University of North Carolina Chapel Hill–Wilson Library.
Thanks for the continuing support of Barbara Springs, Andrew Martin, Mary Kay Forbes, Glenn Bolick, Jim and Judy Dollar, Connie Mason, Frances Eubanks.
Thanks to Christine Riley, Sara San Angelo, Kate Everingham, Marissa Foster, and Douglas Rogers at Arcadia Publishing.
Thanks to Mark Berry of the College of Charleston for setting me on this important quest.

INTRODUCTION

Columbia's beginnings were not haphazard. The original town was created formally and officially by a vote of the state legislature and was laid out according to a pre-conceived plan. As a capital city, much of its history and folklore are connected with the growth and progress of the entire state of South Carolina. The influx of hundreds of legislators have always had a yearly and seasonal altering of the news, real estate, political thought, overall progress, and the future of the area.

My mother and I have many memories. We both grew up as Columbia grew and our points of view span 88 years. Some may say we are armchair historians when in actuality we are eyewitnesses to and participants in the growth of a great place. I combined research of recorded history, journals, interviews with native Columbians, and letters with our personal photograph collection and our personal impressions of the city, the places we knew, and the people we remember.

Margaret Wright Autrey was born on May 7, 1915, the day the *Lusitania* sank. She remains sharp on the details of turn of the century life. In her day, Columbia was the city that had grown from the Reconstruction years. She walked by the houses that escaped Sherman's burning and the Reconstruction buildings on her way to school every day. She remembers when Chicora College was in the Hampton-Preston House. She was a student at Taylor School in 1921 and was among the first group of young Columbians to get a "modern public education." She recalls what it was like to wear bloomers, middy blouses, and cotton stockings in P.E. class. She also wore a bathing costume, rather than a swimsuit. She remembers her mother daring to wear a skirt baring her ankle rather than one that "swept up the sidewalk."

In the 1910s and early 1920s, Columbia was a pedestrian city. Automobiles were a luxury for wealthy citizens. The regular folk rode the streetcar or hailed a "jitney." The broad avenues beckoned the city kids to play in the street; however, games were mostly played on the sidewalk or on the side of the street; ball was played in a backyard or on a vacant lot. Young Margaret and her friends roller-skated to school, because Columbia was ahead of its time with paved sidewalks.

Mother was the only child of Theodore, a retired police officer, and Lilly, who worked at the Columbia Bakery on Main Street. They first lived on Gregg Street on the edge of the downtown near the Southern Railroad Shops. The Eleazers were neighbors and owned a magnificent two-story house with their grocery store next door. Their daughter, Ethel, was 19, but she took up a lot of time with young Margaret. My mother thought Ethel was beautiful and followed her around "like a puppy." They spent hours sitting on the front steps singing World War I songs like "Over There." The family had a huge dining room table and mother was often invited to a boarding house style dinner.

Later, the Autrey family moved to Main Street to make it easier for Lilly to walk to work. Main Street was the center of activity. It was exciting for young Margaret to walk up and down the street with her mother and window shop on balmy evenings. They weren't alone; many of the city's residents strolled as part of their after supper constitutional.

My mother was in the first class at Wardlaw Junior High, the first junior high school in Columbia. She graduated from Columbia High School in 1932 during the Great Depression. Even then, Columbia High School's graduating class had over 300, and the ceremony was held in the Township Auditorium.

My grandmother, Lilly, worked long hours. Mr. Sam Zusman, the bakery owner, was an Orthodox Jew. On Saturdays, the Jewish Sabbath, she worked until late at night. She was there to take care of business as long as there were baked goods and patrons coming by. My grandfather was laid off during the Depression and the family felt fortunate to have bread to eat and have at least one member of the family with a paying job.

When mother married my father, Frank Sims, in 1933, most women didn't drive and families were lucky to have one car. My mother was determined to be ahead of her time. It strengthened her resolve when my father didn't think women should drive and said, "anyway, a woman can't learn to use a straight shift." Mother's friend, Betsy Plourde, took her to Camp Jackson to practice. At the time, there was nothing there except miles of run down shacks. The base was only used in the summer for National Guard training. After driving every day for two weeks, mother went to the highway department. She was asked to drive around the block—no parking required. She paid 60¢ for a metal dog tag license and hung it on her key ring. Her fee for driver's education was paying for Mrs. Plourde's license; she had never gotten one.

I was born in 1947 in the Baptist Hospital—in the old hospital. By then, Columbia had grown by leaps and bounds, but it was still locked in a rigid system of southern traditions. The 1950s and early 1960s were a time when people who met for the first time might still be asked, "Who is your mother's family?" With a name like "Salsi," I'd be immediately identified as an outsider; however, mentioning my maiden name "Sims" and/or my mother as an "Autrey" would prove my roots. Even if no one knew my parents, having an ordinary, non-exotic southern sounding name would help avoid a comment like, "You're not from around here, are you?" During my high school years, my friends referred to Columbia as a "one-horse town." Most of them left to attend college and then sought their fortunes elsewhere. I hung in to graduate from the University of South Carolina and then stayed on for 35 years.

I owned a small business from 1969 to 1984 and was one of the first women to serve on the Greater Columbia Chamber of Commerce Board of Directors. I have fond memories of working as the Belk Fashion Director, working with Miriam Ford at Berry's On Main, producing fashion shows all over town, working on the Christmas Parade Committee, seeing Lou Kaplan and Frank Harris perform at the Town Theatre, having a radio show at WCOS with Woody Windham, and teaching modeling (and manners) to hundreds of

Margaret Autrey is posed in front of the Palmetto Tree Monument on the west side of the front portico of the state capitol building c. 1931.

Columbia teenagers. That was the time that Joe Pinner, Woody Windham, John Wrisley, and Bill Benton were media "fixtures."

I never thought about not living in Columbia, because I never left—completely. My son, Jay, was born in Columbia, spent his elementary school years at Timmerman School, and returned after high school to attend USC. He stayed and married Maria, a Columbia girl. I've spent the past 18 years commuting between Greensboro and Columbia.

My mother and I have always thought of Columbia as "our town." I owned a business on Lady Street, then on Richland, and later on Marion Street for almost 20 years, then I married and moved to North Carolina. Eighteen years, three children, ten plays, and eight books later, my mother relentlessly reminded me that I had not written a book about Columbia.

During this new millennium, Columbia continues to stretch, grow, and attract new families. Unlike the days in the 1950s, when there were few Northerners arriving, except through an association with Fort Jackson or when recruited by industry, Columbia has become an open urbane bastion of civility where those with ideas and energy can flourish, despite the place of their birth. Unlike many historic towns, Columbians do not live with the past as a daily part of their present. Yet thanks to the efforts of preservation societies, museums, universities, and archives, a clear picture remains to illustrate the importance of yesterday on today.

It is with great pleasure that I add storytelling to the facts, figures, and history of the city in my quest to connect and chronicle our common heritage. For Columbia is part of a bond that connects the history of the entire state of South Carolina every time the legislature has convened since 1786.

I hope this book will make you think about your own history. It is important!

Lynn Sims Salsi
March 2003

NOTE: All of the photographs, post cards, and *Harper's Weekly* engravings are from the personal collections of Margaret Autrey Sims and Lynn Sims Salsi, unless otherwise noted below the image.

Lynn Sims led the Belk Young Columbia Council in 1967. High school representatives were photographed in their uniforms on the State House steps.

1. THE LAND ON THE RIVER

The land in the geographic center of South Carolina was generally overlooked for decades after the settling of the Carolina colony at Charles Town. The first known inhabitants were wandering Native Americans, who were members of the Congaree and Wateree tribes. They inhabited seasonal villages and accessed the rivers for transportation. They grew crops in the rich soil near the waterways; miles and miles of open land served as their hunting grounds. During the early 1700s, only a trickle of Europeans came to live in the wilderness areas that became known as the up-country in the middle of the state and the back-country in the northwestern foothills and mountains. Therefore, the history of the piedmont area through 1760 is mostly shrouded in mystery.

The English settlers first learned about the Native Americans in Carolina through the drawings of John White, who traveled to the coast of Manteo, North Carolina in 1585. Regardless of the fears surrounding the native people, in the century that followed British opportunists diligently sought to settle Carolina. Their first successful long-term venture was the establishment of Charles Town. New arrivals sought to befriend the Native Americans, who in turn taught the white people how to survive in a rugged environment that offered no niceties or conveniences.

On March 24, 1663, eight supporters of King Charles II of England gained the exclusive right to sell, distribute, and govern the land they named Carolina. They became known as the Lords Proprietors. In order of their names on the charter, they were the Earl of Clarendon, the Duke of Albemarle, Lord Craven, Lord Berkeley, Lord Ashley, Sir George Carteret, Sir William Berkeley, and Sir John Colleton. Their visions of grandeur included gaining power, establishing a new nobility, and increasing their fortunes. They were also united in the idea of establishing an aristocratic colony based on English customs and laws.

Anthony Ashley Cooper, the most prominent proprietor, acted as the leader of the Lords' interest. In 1669, John Locke, a philosopher and Cooper's personal physician, assisted in drawing up the Fundamental Constitution of Carolina. The 128 articles in the document were based on English principles. It set forth an executive council of noblemen along with official representatives of the Lords Proprietors. Ordinary colonists were barred from participation in the government assembly unless they owned 500 acres or more.

Carolina was divided into six 480,000 acre counties. Forty percent of each area was reserved for the Proprietors and the new nobility that was to invest in the New World and form a class of landed gentry. The remaining 60 percent of the land was set aside for settlers. They could apply for a headright of 100–150 acres. Slaveholders were allowed an additional land grant for each slave.

An agreement was drawn up between the Lords Proprietors in 1674 requiring each to pay for a share of supplies for the Charles Town settlement on the Ashley River. Sir William Berkeley failed to pay his share of the venture and the other proprietors bought his interest. The Lords envisioned a land-rush and looked forward to cashing in on tax collections through importing and exporting products. However, none of the Proprietors ever saw the wild and untamed land that was placed in their jurisdiction because they never visited. They appointed representatives including a governor to handle land sales and carry out government business.

They quickly found that it was not easy to recruit either gentry or ordinary people. Those crossing the Atlantic and those emigrating from northern New World towns in Virginia and Pennsylvania were reluctant to relocate to totally unsettled back woods areas that were only traversed by Native Americans, hunters, and ruffians. Although there were a few adventurous men who traveled into the wild land for hunting and trading with the Indians, most people sought to establish their family in an organized community inhabited by people of the same nationality and religious beliefs.

The promise of vast acres for the taking was extremely enticing at a time when land in Europe was hard to come by except through inheritance. It was nearly impossible for

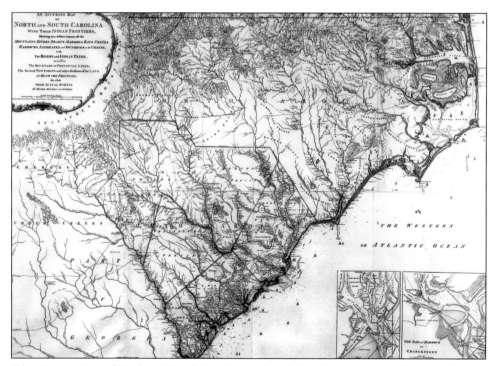

The Mouzan Map of North and South Carolina with its Indian Frontiers was widely used 50 years after its original publication in 1775. Both the British and the American officers used it druing the Revolutionary War.

the average and below average man to obtain property. Therefore, the fact that the land was cheap was a good reason for taking risks to immigrate, even though resettlement in an unknown area was potentially backbreaking and life threatening. Those who ventured forth generally felt that they would find a better life, land, and security. When land sales did not meet the Lords Proprietors expectations, concessions were offered. Robert Horne, a London publisher, printed a pamphlet for the Lords Proprietors entitled *A Brief Description of The Province of Carolina*. It was a report of "an attractive land with salubrious climate and fertile soil." It included a statement of concessions "Promising religious and political right to people settling in the Carolina Province."

Other published inducements included full and free "Liberty of Conscience," freedom from customs on "wine, silk, raisens, currance, oyl, and almonds for 7 years." Every free man and free woman that transported themselves and their servants by March 25, 1667, was granted 100 acres of land for each member of the family and menservants. They were also granted 50 acres for every woman servant and slave. The tax rate was set to be no more than one-half pence per acre, per year. Men were required to be armed with a "good Musquet full bore, 10 pounds of powder, 20 pounds of Bullets, and six months Provision for all, to serve them whilst they raise provision in that Country."

There was encouragement "for those whose Spirit is elevated above the common sort, and for those not afraid to leave his Native Soil to advance his Fortunes equal to his Blood and Spirit. Here with a few Servants and a small Stock a great Estate may be raised, although his Birth has not entitled him to any of the Land of his Ancestors." This was a tempting offer for young men trapped by the law of primogeniture. They could establish their own estate regardless of the order of their birth.

Upon arriving in the New World, a potential landowner petitioned the governor's office and was issued a warrant authorizing a surveyor to stake out a tract. The surveyor's map was returned to the governor's office for approval before the grant was issued. The process was easy, except it did not take long for the average person to realize that the wealthy settlers were acquiring great acreage because they had numbers of servants.

Over decades, notices were regularly posted in towns and villages throughout England and also in the London newspaper. One such announcement published in a 1681 issue of the *True Protestant Mercury* in London proclaimed:

> All those who intend to go as Passengers to Carolina, with Families or without; or, those that desire to be entertained as Servants, may repair with speed to the Sign of the Barbadoes in Finch Lane near the Royal Exchange where they may be informed by the Governor, and the Commanders of the Ships, of the conveniency for their Passage, and the advantage of that Healthful and Plentiful Country.

The first colonial settlements outside of Charles Town eventually brought immigrants seeking farmland and traders who heard about the abundant wild life. These first people scattered throughout South Carolina's regions in search of cheap land, natural resources, and freedom from government interference. People were initially restricted by dangerous roads that were barely wide enough for a horse and rider. They were narrow dirt Indian paths winding through deep forests or paths worn down by migrating animals. As European travelers widened the original paths, new European residents gradually replaced the Native Americans.

The Great Wagon Road, also known as the "bad road," began as a path and was used as early as 1720. Settlers traveled "the road" from North Carolina, Virginia, and Pennsylvania. The path was often impassible as the new landowners struggled to walk or progress in a horse drawn conveyance with all of their worldly goods. Even in good weather, the settlers could only progress about 10 miles a day. In 1744, the English made a treaty with the Iroquois Nation and gained control of the path. By then, it extended from Lancaster, Pennsylvania, through the Shenandoah Valley of Virginia, through the states of North and South Carolina, and ended in Augusta, Georgia.

In 1700, King Charles II named John Lawson the Royal Surveyor General. Lawson was assigned the task of exploring and surveying Carolina. His findings were published to introduce Europeans to the wonders of the New World and to help encourage people to travel to Carolina. He met many native tribes throughout his journey, starting in Charleston and heading through the up-country near where Columbia would later be founded. He traveled north to Charlotte and then east all the way to the North Carolina coast.

Lawson found peaceful tribes who based their societies on fishing, hunting, and gathering. They mostly settled on streams and rivers and were mindful of their environment. In 1700, he recorded information about the midlands, referring to the area as Congaree Town:

> The Indian Kings were always entertaining Travellers, either English or Indian; taking it as a great Affront, if they pass by their Cabins, and take up their Quarters at any other Indian's House. The Queen set Victuals before us, which good Compliment they use generally as soon as you come under their Roof.
>
> The Town consists not of above a dozen Houses, they having other stragling [sic] Plantations up and down the Country. . . . These Indians are a small People, having lost much of their former numbers, by intestine Broils: but most by the Small-pox, which hath often visted them, sweeping away whole towns.
>
> The Congarees are kind and affable to the English, the Queen being very kind, giving us what Rarities her Cabin afforded, as Loblolly made with Indian Corn, and dry's Peaches.

In 1709, Lawson published his findings in a book entitled *A New Voyage to Carolina; Containing the Exact Description and Natural History of the Country: Together with the Present State thereof, and A Journal of a Thousand Miles, Travel'd Thro' Several Nations of Indians, Giving a Particular Account of the Customs, Manners.*

There were good reports about the friendly Indians. (There were 29 tribes scattered throughout the state.) Hunters drawn to the wilderness to obtain pelts for trading established a few dwellings and more families moved in. The land originally referred to as the up-country in the center of the state was bypassed as people settled in the western back-country area in the mountains.

Increased trading, commerce, and the need for supplies called for the establishment of a place to facilitate trade with the Indians and to enable the shipment of goods to communities on the river. A fort was built in 1718 on the western shore of the Congaree

Before Columbia was established, farms and plantations dotted the landscape adjacent to both sides of the rivers. Chopping out cotton was a particularly laborious task.

River at Granby. It was garrisoned for the protection of goods, settlers, and travelers and became an important destination. Paths led to the fort from Charles Town. A trader could take the path known as the Congaree Path and follow the east bank of Four Holes Swamp, passing north of Orangeburg. After reaching the Congaree River, traders followed the west bank of the river to Granby. From Granby the path to Ninety Six was much used, for it led to the Indian town of Keowee. The route served the Cherokee Indians and was also much used by British and American troops during the Revolution. Despite this activity, within a period of 20 years, a few brave pioneers established large farms on the high ground east and west of the river.

Robert Johnson was appointed governor in 1677. Johnson was eventually relieved of his duties, but was re-appointed royal governor after the King took control in 1719, making it a royal colony. At this point, Carolina was divided into "North" and "South" with the Lords Proprietors returning their interest in South Carolina to the King. By 1730, Johnson devised a township plan to attract settlers. He hoped that the formation of towns would encourage people to continue coming and would discourage the Indians from violence.

The governor set up 10,000 to 20,000 acre townships with farms set around. The colony offered 50 acres of land for every family member willing to travel to the unsettled areas. He waived land taxes for ten years along with offering a food and equipment bounty for two years. The free equipment was an important incentive especially for those traveling from Europe. Settlers were limited in the amount of property that they could bring. Poorer classes of immigrants sometimes only brought the clothing on their backs along with what little they could carry.

Johnson's plan was successful for a 10 year period between 1730 and 1740. By then, several areas had an established landed upper class. Approximately 2,500 people arrived from Germany, Switzerland, and the British Isles. Most landed in Charles Town and then continued up the Santee and Congaree Rivers because those communities located near major waterways were the most successful. Saxe Gotha , a community developed near Granby, attracted many German people.

When the royal government failed to pay the promised bounties, it created hardships. By 1740, the lack of funds and the uncertainty brought by the escalating friction, which eventually resulted in the French and Indian War, discouraged people who were interested in obtaining land. James Glen was appointed royal governor from 1743 to 1756. His goal was to make peace with the Native Americans in order to promote new settlements. When the Indian War broke out in the back-country, he was replaced.

Every aspect of developing the new territory was connected with relationships with the Native Americans. For the most part, the state of affairs with the various tribes was not taken for granted. In 1763, Governor Glenn wrote, in *A Description of the Province of South Carolina*:

> The concerns for this country are so closely connected and interwoven with Indian affairs, and not only a great branch of our trade, but even the safety of the Province, do so much depend upon our continuing in friendship with the Indians, that I thought it highly necessary to gain all the knowledge I could of them.

The events surrounding the French and Indian War forced Scotch-Irish in Pennsylvania, who were concerned about Indian attacks, to move south. They ventured south of Charlotte to land that was once owned by the Waxhaw Indians and formed a Presbyterian Church. The area known as the Waxhaws became the first land in the back-country to be settled. This community on the border of North and South Carolina made it easier for others to follow and to move even further south. The influx of settlers and the uncertainty of war caused the Fort at Granby to be refurbished and enlarged in 1748.

As settlers pushed from the north and south, the Native Americans migrated further west to the mountainous upcountry and away from the people coming to clear and cultivate farmland. By then, the Indian population was reduced by one-half, mostly from diseases brought from Europe. With the western migration of Native Americans, the governor set a boundary and declared that no white settlers could settle beyond the line. The area beyond the line was known as Indian Country.

Eventually, the rolling land and rivers of the midlands were found to be a natural gateway to the back-country. However, people did not arrive in droves. They were not accustomed to vast dense forests. The European landscape of the 1700s had a cultivated appearance and the Carolina forests were anything but civilized. The way of life was brutal. New settlers literally had to live off the land.

Those who came to live in the center of the state relied on the vast virgin forests for subsistence, the rivers for transportation, and the plentiful wild game for food. Additionally, there was cheap plentiful land, a long growing season, and a temperate climate. Once removed, the trees were used for houses, fuel, transportation, furnishings, and fences. The cleared land was fertile and grew a variety of crops. Mills were established on the waterways and sawn lumber became available for clapboard houses. The wood products added to the economic stability of the area. Bark from the red oak trees was vital to the leather trade and became a source of tannin for treating hives. Mills were constructed to grind the bark into "tanbark."

The settlers who lived "in the middle of nowhere" received the same disdainful treatment as those in the mountain back-country. They were accorded no respect, had no courts, no jails, no representation in the Commons House, and were charged the same taxes for their land as the wealthy planters in Charles Town. Those in the mountains feared both the Native Americans and roaming plunderers. They eventually took the law into their own hands when their pleas to the politicians in Charles Town went unheeded. With no help forthcoming and no protection, hundreds of citizens banded together and expelled robbers and horse thieves.

The section became known as a place of compromise when a petition signed by 4,000 back-country settlers caused the legislature to pass the Circuit Court Act of 1768. The province was split into circuit court districts of Charles Town, Beaufort, Georgetown, Cheraw, Camden, Orangeburg, and Ninety Six for the purpose of providing easier access to courts.

The northern regions became known as a healthy area where low-country residents

The geographic center of the state attracted settlers because the waterways made excellent sites for mills. Overshot water wheels supplied the power for many of the early mills.

could escape fevers and diseases of the marshy, warm, and more populated towns. Many ordinary low-country farmers moved away from the coastal misery, miasma, and swamps. However, most of the permanent residents of the state's mid-section came from Virginia, North Carolina, Pennsylvania, and northern colonies where towns were crowded and where land prices had escalated.

Two families arrived who impacted the history of the area for over a century. John Taylor came to the midlands of South Carolina from Virginia in 1749 with his sons Thomas and James. He purchased thousands of acres of land. There is a widespread legend that he traded a gun and a horse for a parcel of land. In a time when cash was not the prevailing currency in a little inhabited area, a trade in kind could have been arranged. Taylor and his sons cleared, constructed, and erected a house at Black Swamp. Later, Thomas and James established two large plantations on the east side of the Congaree River—"The Plains" and "Richland."

When Thomas Taylor married Ann Wyche, they first settled near Granby. Their first son, John, was born in 1770. Thomas established sound political connections and served in 1775 in the First Provincial Congress. This began his career in politics and community service that lasted until the day he died. About this time, Taylor joined Timothy Reves and Wade Hampton I in obtaining a grant for 18,150 acres of land across the Congaree in the Camden District. In 1775, Thomas was a captain in the third regiment of the South Carolina line and was commissioned to receive signatures for the Continental Association, which pledged citizens to bear arms in defense of the province. When politics heated up in

Much of the land on the Saluda and Congaree Rivers remained undeveloped for decades after the Revolutionary War. The river land was sought after for the establishment of large farms. Early visitors commented on the forests and fields that were close by, even after Columbia was laid out.

Colonel Thomas Taylor's son Henry Pendleton Taylor was born in Columbia. He married Ann Trezvant of Charleston and later moved his family to the low-country.

Charles Town and a war was imminent, he resigned his commission in 1777.

Wade Hampton I arrived in Columbia about 1776, when he was 24 years old. His young years were spent in the Waxhaw area of South Carolina. While he was away, Cherokees massacred his family. When Charles Town fell to the British in May 1780, Wade Hampton and Thomas Taylor joined the militia. They both also served together in the newly formed legislature. During the war, Hampton escaped from a British prison and fought with General Thomas Sumter. His first wife, Martha Howells, was a wealthy widow. She predeceased him and left him hundreds of acres of land near the Taylors' plantations including Greenfield Plantation in the Richland district. He remained in the area by adding to his large holdings, and in time he became a very wealthy man.

In 1785, Wade and his brother Richard Hampton purchased the right to operate the ferry across the Congaree River. The first ferry operation was begun in 1754 by Martin Friday. It became known as "Friday's Ferry" and connected Granby and Saxe Gotha on the west bank with the farms on higher ground across the Congaree River. This provided a much needed convenience and greater access to travelers through the area to the seat of government in Charles Town in the south and to Charlotte, North Carolina in the north.

By the 1760s, a permanent bridge across the Congaree was necessary to encourage commerce and development. With the increased traffic of people and commerce, a ferry was no longer adequate. Wade Hampton I attempted to construct a bridge in 1771; however, high water and flooding hampered the project. The Revolutionary War ultimately brought his efforts to a halt and the ferry continued as the only mode of transportation across the river.

There were few communities in the midlands, even by 1780. Camden, 20 miles to the west, was the site of a strategic Revolutionary battle. Granby had a trading post that was established about 1765 by James Chestnut and Joseph Kershaw. It was a three-story frame building that was used as a store and a residence and was located on the banks of the river. The structure ultimately passed to the Cayce family through marriage and became known as the Cayce house.

With the fort as a stronghold, the area became an established market area. As the Revolutionary War heated up, British troops were ordered to march from Charleston to North Carolina. With the battle of Camden came skirmishes fought hand-to-hand guerilla-style throughout the area. The British established a palisade at Granby and took over the ferry. That gave them control of the area's most important supply route: the river.

Until that time, the few residents of the up-country had no thoughts about war. They looked upon the injustices inflicted by the British as a problem of the low-country planters and politicians. The up-country and back-country planters' petitions for representation in the colonial legislature had been ignored by the royal governor and overlooked by low-country planters. They were content to ignore the war until the reconnoitering British troops wreaked havoc on their fields and homes. The marching, ravaging soldiers got their attention.

The trading area proved to be a pawn in the struggles between the British and the Patriots. Both wanted access to the navigable waters and trade routes. In 1781, the fort and Cayce house fell back into the hands of the British.

After the Battle of Ninety-Six, Nathanael Greene's army of 1,000 retreated south toward the Congarees. They were followed by 2,000 British commanded by General Francis Rawdon. Greene encamped near the Wateree River while Rawdon was at the Granby fort. Greene was cut off from General Thomas Sumter. Since it was deemed impossible to get a man through the enemy lines to warn Sumter, 18-year-old Emily Geiger, the daughter of a local farmer, volunteered to deliver a message to Sumter. Emily was intercepted by Rawdon's scouts and taken to the Cayce house. While waiting for a Tory matron to search her, Emily memorized General Greene's orders and then ate the paper. She was released and resumed a route to Sumter's camp. She arrived safely and Sumter hastened to reinforce Greene. On May 15, 1781, Patriot forces under the command of Light Horse Harry Lee routed the British and recaptured the fort at Granby. Colonel Thomas Taylor was placed in command of the post.

By the end of the war, the state was devastated. Nevertheless, the land in the center of the state was becoming a crossroads for people traveling north and south and became a gathering point for farmers seeking a market. Troop movements had widened many paths and packed them down into roads. War-weary soldiers familiar with the area spread the word about the abundant natural resources and the availability of land. Post-war newcomers sought land near the well-known areas of Saxe Gotha and Granby. The land was fertile, flat, easy to till, cheap, and near swiftly flowing rivers. The temperate climate offered a long growing season that favored most crops, except for Sea Island cotton and rice.

The lack of an organized banking system and a medium of exchange was critical. Crops failed in 1784 and 1785 and creditors pressured debtors to repay loans. South Carolina citizens experienced difficulty in organizing financing until 1791, when President George Washington approved a bill to charter the Bank of the United States. It did not help that all residents of the state had to travel to a court district and sometimes all the way to Charleston to conduct business.

All of this led to a serious movement for changing the seat of government. There were heated and continuing debates throughout the state. Many people felt that progress and expansion would be stymied as long as the center of government was not centrally located. As the farthermost points in the state became settled, ordinary residents found it impossible to travel the great distance on foot or by horse-drawn conveyance to a distant district court for recording legal transactions. Land grants had to be registered there no matter where the property was located in the state. Citizens also pushed for the adaptation of a new state constitution made by a convention of the people. Moving the capital to the interior was long overdue.

Richland County was created as a concession to the pressure of up-country and back-country residents in 1785. Those in the up-country snubbed by the low-country residents resented being excluded from affairs of state. They pushed for a new constitution to guarantee them participation in government, to abolish religious discrimination, and to develop additional courts. Therefore, the land in the Camden District bordered on the west by the piedmont, on the northeast by the Pee Dee River, and on the east and southeast by the coastal area became a new county. It was carved from Camden County and extended northwest to southeast for almost 50 miles and averaged 16 miles in width.

The Cayce House was one of the first structures on the west bank of the Congaree River near Friday's Ferry. A store was located on the first floor to serve early traders and settlers. Emily Geiger was held prisoner in a second floor bedroom.

21

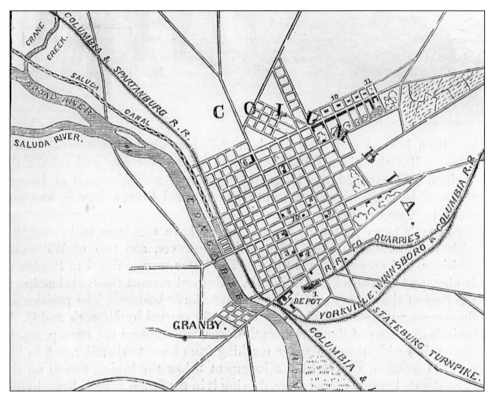

Columbia became the seat of government in the geographic center of the state through compromise. It was bordered on the west by rivers and on the south by swampland.

Richland probably received its name from the richness of the land that lay along the banks of the Saluda, Wateree, and Broad Rivers that flowed through its boundaries.

In 1783, General Thomas Sumter proposed the state government relocate to Stateburgh on the Santee River in an area known as the "high hills" that was close to his home. Low-country politicians dragged their feet as long as possible. The general assembly elected a committee to investigate the feasibility of a move two years later. The total power of government was in the low-country and those who lived there were reluctant to see their capital move away. They were more reluctant to have a new center of government with amenities that would threaten the status of Charles Town.

The Santee River location was found to be near swamps and the location was rejected on March 1, 1786. Camden was recommended, as was level land on the west side of the Congaree River near Lexington. John Lewis Gervais, a Charleston merchant, was supportive of the recommendation to locate the capital on the high ground of the Taylor Plantation on the east side of the river. When the land near Lexington flooded after a downpour, it was dropped from consideration. The official vote was taken on March 22, 1786. The Taylor land, near Friday's Ferry, won by one vote.

On March 29, 1786, an act of the General Assembly appointed commissioners to purchase the land:

for the purpose of building a town, and for removing the seat of Government thereto. Whereas the continuing of the seat of government in the City of Charleston is productive of many inconveniences and great expense to the citizens of this State for the remedy whereof.

The act directed commissioners to lay off a tract of land of 2 miles square near Friday's Ferry on the Congaree River, "including the plain of the hill whereon Thomas and James Taylor Esquires now reside, into lots of half an acre each." When ratified, the bill was "An Act to appoint Commissioners to purchase Land for the purpose of building a Town, and for removing the Seat of Government thereto."

The Seibels House is still standing as one of the oldest in Columbia. It was built for Colonel Thomas Taylor's daughter and originally stood on the edge of town on his plantation land. The house and property are now part of the Columbia Preservation Society. (Photo by Burke Salsi.)

2. A New State Capital

"Taylor's Hill" lay on the east bank, where the Broad and the Saluda Rivers joined to form the Congaree River. The tract for the new town was cut from Colonel Thomas Taylor's cotton plantation. The five commissioners elected by joint ballot of the Senate and House of Representatives to plan the new town included Colonel Thomas Taylor, Alexander Gillon of Charleston, Judge Henry Pendleton of Saxe Gotha, General Richard Winn of Winnsborough, and Colonel Richard Hampton of Saxe Gotha. They were authorized to lay off the tracts and set aside public areas. The property was subdivided into lots of one-half an acre with four lots per block. State Statute at Large IV further stated that after the lots were sold, the price should be paid to the owners of the land out of the first proceeds from the sale.

Their first duty was to lay out a town that would be suitable for a seat of government. Each man was required to give a personal bond of £5,000. In return, they were allowed a commission of two and one-half percent on the sale of the lots. John Gabriel Guignard of Stateburgh was the surveyor. He had the task of exacting the layout of the town. He established order and function in his plans that are still evident today. Guignard was exempt from the bond and was paid for his services. At the time, he purchased vast acreage on the west side of the river near Granby. The commissioners also made many suggestions that permanently affected the future physical development of the town. Dr. Edward Fisher served on the committee that purchased the land. It was also fortuitous that he was a physician and became the first doctor in the area.

Careful attention was given to the layout of streets. The state statute required them to be at least 60 feet wide. The broad thoroughfares gave the town a fine appearance, but more practically the wide streets also impeded the spread of disease. Two principle streets, Assembly and Senate, were to be 150 feet wide and run though the center of the town at right angles. Streets to the west and perpendicular to Assembly Street were named for Revolutionary War Continental Army generals who served in South Carolina. The north-south streets were named for products including rice, tobacco, indigo, and wheat. Upper Boundary Street, Lower Boundary Street, Harden Street, and the Congaree River were defined as the city limits.

Two public squares were set aside and named in honor of John Rutledge and General William Moultrie. Rutledge was the first governor of South Carolina after the royal governor returned to England. Moultrie was the defender of Charles Town during the

Revolution and the ranking officer of South Carolina when the act was ratified to create the new capital. Columbia automatically became part of Richland County. The county was divided into five sections designated by topography—Piedmont, Sand Hill, Red Hill, River Bottom, and River Terrace.

Property was set aside for a State House building. It was a square located in the middle of Richardson Street with Gervais Street perpendicular on the north and Senate Street perpendicular on the south. This decision caused Richardson Street (later renamed Main Street) to displace Assembly Street as the main north-south route. The wide street running from the ferry crossing on the river and crossing in front of the State House was named Gervais Street in honor of John Lewis Gervais. Plans for a proper building facing Gervais Street included a two-story wooden structure. The building's designer, James Hoban, later became famous for his design of the White House in Washington, D.C.

One-fifth of the lots were to be sold to the highest bidder at "not less than 20 pounds each." Money raised from the sale of the property financed the construction of the State House. It had rooms for the General Assembly, courts, and offices for public officials. The sale of the lots was advertised in the *State Gazette* and the *Charleston Morning Post and Daily Advertiser* in Charleston. The first sale held in Charleston on September 2, 1786, attracted families, politicians, and investors. The name of each purchaser was hand written on a map. The commissioners used it as an official record of sales until Columbia was incorporated in 1806.

The act took care of the appearance of the new town. Those buying lots were required "to build thereon a frame, wood, stone, or brick house, not less than thirty feet long and

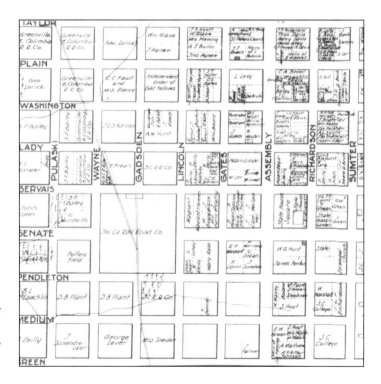

From the beginning, Columbia was a planned town. State House Square now encompasses both blocks originally bisected by Richardson Street (now Main Street).

eighteen feet in the clear, with brick or stone chimneys, within the space of three years from the time of such purchase." Thomas and James Taylor and other landowners that had dwellings within the 2-mile limit were permitted to reserve 2 acres each on their own property. However, they had to agree to only build additions in a manner consistent with the plan of the town.

The call to make the physical move of the government offices came in 1789, when the new State House building was ready for occupancy. At the December session in Charles Town, Governor Charles Pinckney requested that the General Assembly meet at the new State House on the first Monday of January 1790. A report from the town commissioners to the governor indicated that accommodations were ready for 217 people and that there would be stabling for 310 horses. A market was built and furnished with provisions. In the meantime, the General Assembly transferred the public records as the buildings were being completed.

When the first session convened in January, the state house was complete and included wells and privies to serve the members. There were no lodgings built for the legislature, therefore the members had to find lodging in private homes and taverns on both sides of the river. Thomas Taylor offered his house for accommodations; the governor was among those staying with the Taylors. However, the new capital was a place with no name and was referred to as "Friday's Ferry" or "Taylor's Hill."

At the session, the governor called for a constitutional convention that finally fulfilled the 40-year-old demands of the up-country and back-country residents. A Charleston newspaper reported there would be "no sermons, balls, or oyster pies." Even though a new constitution was adopted and signed on June 3, 1790, there was a continuation of the old arguments concerning the new location. The politicians and gentry of the low-country

The first State House building of 1790 was designed by James Hoban, designer of the White House. It was a two-story wooden building on a square of land that was set aside by the legislature.

were reluctant to give up control of the decisions of the state. The delegates stuck to their decision about the new location, yet a compromise was made for sharing power between the up-country and the low-country. One of the provisions included appointing two state treasurers—one in Columbia and one in Charles Town. Other state officials, including the surveyor-general and the secretary of state, were required to keep two offices, one in each town. The Court of Appeals also met in both places. The governor, however, agreed to remain in Columbia during the legislative sessions.

After that, the new capital was officially approved and a motion was made to name the town. The name "Columbia" was selected as a tribute to Christopher Columbus. Finally, the constitution was ratified and the convention adjourned. The first noteworthy visitor to the new community was President George Washington. He arrived in 1791 as part of his southern tour to visit Revolutionary War sites. In his journal, he described the town as "an uncleared wood with very few houses on it, and these all wooden ones." He referred to the State House as "commodious but unfinished." There was no official residence for the governor, so Washington stayed in a private home.

In the beginning, the state legislature made all the decisions for Columbia with suggestions from the commissioners. However, when the general assembly was in recess, Colonel Thomas Taylor, James Taylor, William Montgomery, George Wade, and Benjamin Waring acted as the governing body. Citizens used the State House building for bazaars, dances, and community events. The well-to-do staged grand balls. Other local social activities included horseracing and gambling. The special events helped to attract visitors and investors to the area and caused politicians and plantation owners to build second homes in town.

The landed politicians also brought prestige and influence. Many of the legislators were well-known Revolutionary War heroes, including Wade Hampton I and Thomas Taylor. Colonel William A. Washington, a native Virginian, was also among the celebrated. After the war, he moved to Charleston and served both Charleston and Colleton Counties in many capacities including terms in the House of Representatives and the Senate. His presence in Columbia stirred the social scene, especially because of his close relationship with his cousin, George.

The area gradually developed; within seven years the population was great enough for the establishment of a local government with a board of nine commissioners. They created services for the citizens, including the monitoring of streets and markets. They later became an elected board of seven who also had the power to adopt safety regulations and to collect fines.

The opportunities to shape a town out of a forest attracted skilled labor and businessmen. A stagecoach service offered transportation between Charleston and Columbia. Taverns opened, offering refreshments and accommodations to travelers and residents. Timothy Reves built the Reves Tavern on Gervais Street across from the State House in 1792. It was a popular eatery and "watering hole" for legislators. Other businesses included gins, a gristmill, a saw mill, a tannery, tobacco warehouses, cottonseed presses, a castor oil press, a brickyard, a paper mill, and an iron factory. Great capital investments were made in Columbia; however, the progress gave mute testimony to the contribution given by approximately 1,451 slaves. They felled trees, cleared streets, built houses, worked on

The stagecoach was the preferred choice of transportation until the railroad connected Columbia to Charleston and Charlotte. (Courtesy North Carolina Office of Archives and History.)

farms, and ran businesses. An exact figure representing the percentage of free blacks in the city by 1792 is not available. It is apparent that the greatest number would have served as workers and servants for the 2,479 white residents, who included politicians, farmers, and businessmen.

Slaves were also the backbone of developing cash crops and of expanding the plantation system. Planters on the coast were aided by a long growing season and learned to take advantage of the climate by growing rice, tobacco, indigo, and Sea Island cotton, which produced long silky fibers. None of these crops could be propagated in central South Carolina where the weather was colder. Short staple cotton with its aggravating seeds was the variety that grew inland. It was not profitable because it was labor intensive to de-seed. After Eli Whitney invented the cotton gin in 1790, cotton became a cash crop and the mid-state farmers were on the way to wealth. It became possible for farmers to process tens of thousands of acres. Most of it was shipped to Charleston and increased the ties between these areas of the state. The greatest drawback of the invention was the dependency South Carolina developed on agriculture, causing the expansion of slavery.

The new-found wealth showed up in the homes and lifestyles of Columbians. Merchants, brokers, warehouse owners, and opportunists moved to town. Cotton Town was created on the north end of town at Elmwood Avenue. It became the location for brokerage offices and warehouses for over 100 years. As the town became a market center, it became fashionable to own both a country house and a city house. By 1801, there were 100 buildings in the town.

News of George Washington's death in December 1799 reached Columbia. J.H. Guignard, Reverend D.E. Dunlap, Dr. William Montgomery, Joshua Benson, Colonel Thomas Taylor, and R.H. Waring formed a committee on January 18, 1800 to pay tribute to the fallen president. They recommended that:

> the inhabitants of this town and its vicinity, to wear crape on the left arm for thirty days from this time, as a mark of the much lamented loss sustained by their country. It is also recommended, that the citizens meet on the said day, at the house of Major Benson at 11 o'clock a.m. to walk in procession to the State House.

Despite early success, a struggle continued to unite all of the sections of the state. Governor John Drayton urged the legislature to establish a college for young men. He convinced the governing body that a school in the center of the state would attract students from all areas. He felt that having the smartest youth share a common education would unite the sections and factions. The South Carolina College was chartered in 1801 and became the first state college in the United States to be supported by the appropriation of public funds. Colonel Taylor was an avid supporter of the college and was appointed one of the first directors.

A few blocks of wooded land were set aside south of the State House for a campus. Reverend Doctor Jonathon Maxcy of Brown University was named the first president and Enoch Hanford was appointed the only professor. Other brilliant professors followed, including Thomas Cooper, Maximilian LcBorde, John LeConte, and Joseph LeConte. The Rutledge Building, the first structure, served as classrooms, dormitory, living quarters for professors, and a chapel.

The college opened on January 10, 1805 with eight students. Graduates of the college became attorneys, doctors, teachers, ministers, political leaders, military officers, and governors. The Clariosophic and Euphradian Societies were formed and offered debate experience. The college became well known for training orators.

Reverend Maxcy was active in the establishment of the First Baptist Church on Hampton Street in 1809. He accepted the call to be the first minister and baptized the nine white and four black members in the Congaree River.

Edward Hooker came from Connecticut in 1805 to teach at the college. His diary records:

> The township of Columbia is not very large . . . laid out into lots and streets; but not more than one-third of the streets are yet opened; and of those which are opened, several have not more than two or three buildings upon them. The State House is placed on an eminence directly in the center of the township, though very far from the center of the buildings.
>
> That part of the town that is not put into open streets is, for the most part, a wilderness of pines. The State House is very large on the ground, but yet so low as to be entirely void of anything like just proportions. It has only two stories and one of these is partly below the natural surface of the ground. The lower story is appropriated to the Treasurer's, Secretary's, and Surveyor General's offices. There are several other rooms which, as far as I can learn, are used for little else than lodging rooms for the goats that run loose about the streets and which, as the doors are never shut, have at times free access. The courthouse is a much handsomer building, of brick, two stories high.
>
> There is only one church. . . . The people think it is a very neat and pretty building . . . but it has no steeple. The number of houses and stores in town I judge to be over an hundred. The houses are generally built of wood, the chimneys carried up all the way on the outside. They are without cellars being set upon blocks and are unconnected with their kitchens.
>
> As to the ladies fashions, I notice with satisfaction that their dresses are not so immodestly cut and put on, as those of the Northern fashionables.

During the early years, the legislature was most concerned about the building and organization of the town. Among their considerations were building roads, clearing creeks, and establishing taxes to pay for internal improvements. Legislators were concerned about every issue including the moral conduct of its citizens. *The Columbia Gazette* regularly covered proceedings of the legislature. On December 9, 1794, the paper reported that the august body was "praying for a law to pass, for clearing and rendering various creeks and waterways navigable."

An act of the General Assembly in 1801 granted the commissioners of markets the power to license all billiard tables within the town limits. They used the fees to finance the sinking of wells and the purchase of a fire engine. The billiard fee was later set at $500 per table and was payable to the intendant. By December 1822, the legislature had second thoughts about the game. They passed an act limiting the location of billiard tables to within 15 miles of town. The intendant and wardens were not to issue licenses for tables closer to the city limits. There must have been some dissention within the legislative body as the act was soon amended allowing billiards within 5 miles of Columbia during July, August, and September.

The game of billiards was a continuing hot political topic, for Robert Mills wrote about it in his 1826 *Statistics of South Carolina*. He discussed the benefits of banning the tables: "It is evident in the moral habits of the citizens and it is all important, on account of the number of youth being educated at the public institutions in the place."

Columbia was officially incorporated as a town by an act of the legislature in 1805. An intendant and six wardens were elected annually to govern the town. In December of 1808, Thomas Taylor took over as the only commissioner. At this time, the General Assembly passed a statute that also provided for a full-time marshal. He served as the clerk of the town market and was required to go through the town every Sunday to suppress disorder.

John Gabriel Guignard was elected to serve as the treasurer of the upper division and relocated to Columbia full time. In 1801, he became state surveyor general. He purchased a house at the corner of Senate and Pickens that had been built by Revolutionary War hero General Peter Horry. He also established two plantations on his acreage on the west side of the Congaree River—Still Hopes and Rising Hopes. The Saluda Mill, one of the first textile manufacturing mills, was constructed on his property at Rising Hopes in 1832. His son, James Sanders Guignard, became Columbia's postmaster and served as a probate judge in the 1790s. Part of his plantation land remained in the family for over 150 years. Still Hopes is now the site of an Episcopal nursing home.

The first 20 years of growth were slow but steady as society, businesses, industries, educational endeavors, and religious institutions were established. The presence of the state government defined the town and established a permanent hold on Columbia. Columbia was made the county seat of the Richland District in 1799. There is no record stating where the court met in its first 14 years. However, the move made another contribution to the growth of the town. The first courthouse was a two-story structure and was one of the first large buildings in town. It was constructed with a jail, pillory, and stocks, on the northeast corner of Main and Washington Streets. F.W. Williams recorded in *Old and New Columbia* that it was "a much handsomer building than the State House." It was razed in 1850 to make way for a more modern facility that was built on the same site.

The Taylors remained in the new town, made the most of their land investments, and contributed greatly to the religious, social, and political history of Columbia. Colonel Thomas Taylor was well established before the General Assembly voted to move the capital. He and his brother owned several plantations including "the Plains" closest to the new town. The Taylors owned large houses and had slaves to work in the tobacco and cotton fields. After the streets were laid out, Thomas's home was located right on the edge of town at the corner of Richland and Barnwell Streets. He kept his old two-story house. The family burying ground was across the street and the slave graveyard was on the corner of Barnwell and Lumber. The old Taylor spring was a gathering place for family and friends. Many picnics and barbeques were held there.

From the day Columbia was founded until the end of his life, Colonel Taylor was regarded as Columbia's "first citizen." He was literally the first citizen; however, he was also accorded the title out of respect for his service to his state and to his country. In addition to his service on the first state constitution committee and as a town commissioner, he represented the area as a state senator. James Taylor owned the adjoining plantation and after the sale of the property to the state, James built a magnificent new house on the corner of Washington and Marion Streets.

The Taylors did their share in establishing Columbia as a year-round town. In 1785, Colonel Taylor built a home for his daughter, Mrs. A.M. Hale, on a portion of his plantation property near his home. The house was built on a narrow sandy lane before all

The Guignard plantation, Rising Hopes, extended to the river and the Saluda Mill was built on the site. It was the first textile mill in the area and remained in production through the Civil War.

Colonel Peter Horry served under Francis Marion, "the Swamp Fox," during the Revolutionary War and built this house on the corner of Pickens and Senate Streets prior to 1813. John Gabriel Guignard later lived in the house. It is known as the Horry-Guignard House and still stands on the original site. (Photo by Burke Salsi.)

of the streets were laid out. Prior to the Civil War, Ann B. Seibels acquired the house. It is still standing and is considered to be the oldest building in Columbia.

Thomas Taylor's son John built a house on the corner of Laurel and Assembly Streets. The property was high on the hill where the areas of Laurel Hill and Arsenal Hill met. At the time, he lived "out of town," yet he had a clear vista of the river and the entire town all the way to the State House. John was the first intendant of Columbia and in 1826, he was elected the first governor from Columbia. His house survived the burning of Columbia in 1865, but it was destroyed by another fire in 1893.

Thomas Taylor, Sr. was impatient for Columbia to grow and prosper. He witnessed the slow growth of the town and was heard to say, "I've swapped a damned good cotton plantation for a damned poor town." His great, great, great, grandson Talbot Bissell says that he heard about his grandfather's comment all of his life. Taylor lived to be 90 years old and witnessed Columbia as an established capital with over 100 structures. However, it can be noted that by that time of Taylor's death in 1833, there were no buildings east of the South Carolina College except for a few blocks due south of the State House. The area was surrounded by fields and forests.

Church services were held by a circuit-riding preacher about every six weeks at the Taylor home even before the town was established. Reverend Isaac Smith preached there until 1795 when Sunday services were regularly conducted at the State House. The Methodists and the Presbyterians alternated weeks. Colonel Thomas Taylor signed the call for David E. Dunlap, a Methodist minister. Unfortunately, Reverend Dunlap died on September 10, 1804 following the death of his wife Susannah on the same day.

Then Reverend John Harper, ordained by John Wesley, arrived. He began a Methodist Church with six members and preached in the State House until he obtained two lots and built the first church structure in Columbia—the Washington Street Methodist Church. It was considered to be in the woods, even though it was only four blocks off the main thoroughfare. The small wooden structure was replaced with a brick church in 1831.

Colonel Taylor was also active in the beginnings of the Presbyterian Church. In 1813, the legislature passed an act that incorporated "the First Presbyterian Church of the Town of Columbia." It provided for the appraisal of one-half of the old burying ground and instructed that the property be conveyed to the First Presbyterian Church and the Protestant Episcopal Church. Each church was to pay one-half of the appraised value to the Methodists and Baptists to help them complete their churches. The Presbyterians purchased the interest of the Episcopalians after they acquired two acres as a gift. Thomas Taylor, Thomas Lindsay, and John Murphy were elected as the first elders of the church. They salvaged materials from the Granby Courthouse and built a small sanctuary. The building was moved to Lady Street when a new sanctuary was begun in 1851.

A year later, the Episcopalians built on their lot on the east side of the State House. Their wooden structure was replaced by a stately structure modeled after Yorkminster Cathedral in England in 1846. Colonel Edward Brickell White, the designer of the Huguenot Church and the steeple for St. Phillips in Charleston, was the architect and builder.

It was fortunate for Wade Hampton that the government moved only a few miles from his land, for it put him in the center of politics and power. With his great wealth, he quickly became an integral part in the development of the political, business, and social life of Columbia. He never shrank from duty and during the War of 1812, he served as a colonel under Andrew Jackson. He participated in the Battle of New Orleans and afterward was dispatched to tell the news of victory.

Hampton built a new plantation at Woodlands for his second wife, Harriet Flud. He adapted the best inventions of the day for use on his farm, and by 1805 his cotton gins were driven by water. He prospered and at one time had an annual income of $50,000. He again expanded his holdings and eventually owned plantations in Mississippi and Louisiana.

Wade Hampton loved horse racing and raised thoroughbreds and brought racetracks to Columbia. He constructed a personal racetrack on his plantation where he hosted events. By the 1840s, the Hamptons, Singletons, and others established a track south of town. They built a second track known as the Columbia Jockey Club, east of Columbia where Epworth Children's Home was later established. Some of the finest stock in the country was attracted to run at both tracks and Columbia became a regular stop on a prestigious racing circuit.

Abram Blanding came to Columbia from Massachusetts in 1798 to be the first principal of the Columbia Male Academy. It is not known, however, how many students studied with him during his first year in Columbia. He also read law with John Taylor, Thomas Taylor's son. He taught for a year and then moved to Camden to set up a law practice. His first wife was related to U.S. Senator John C. Calhoun and his second wife was the daughter of Chancellor Henry William deSaussure. Therefore, his social position became well established in the state.

There was a need for lawyers to serve in the capital. John Taylor was among the first to practice. He was joined by other young men from various parts of the country who sought the opportunity to practice in a capital that was also a county seat. Among those who came were Thomas Henry Egan from Maryland, John Hooker of Connecticut, and Robert Stark of Virginia. Abraham Nott of Connecticut became the first Columbia attorney elected to a judgeship. He arrived in Columbia in 1804 and became a judge in 1810.

It was not until 1812 that Columbia had a bank. The state treasury remained in Charleston, causing the town to become a center of banking and finance. The legislature chartered the Bank of the State of South Carolina and provided for a branch in Columbia. It was owned entirely by the state until 1835 and provided local facilities for merchants. Profits were used to help reduce the state debts and at the same time provided tax relief for the state's residents.

By 1813, houses were constructed over a broad area of the streets and avenues in Columbia. Politicians, military heroes, and gentry were proud to belong to the growing number of citizens who made Columbia their primary residence. The home that became known as the Hampton Preston House was built in 1818 by Ainsley Hall. He was an English merchant, known as the "Merchant Prince." Hall opened a general store on Richardson Street and also worked as a cotton broker. He married Sarah Cooke Goodwyn; her sizable dowry established Hall in South Carolina society. Their house occupied a full city block and featured a vast garden of rare and beautiful shrubs and flowers. Cedars were imported from Lebanon and other rare flora was brought from other parts of the world.

Wade Hampton wanted to own a town house that would put him in the center of politics, influence, and culture during the legislative sessions. He also felt that the swamps near his plantation were a source of fever and various miasmas in the hot, sweltering, humid summers. In 1823, he searched for a town house and found that none were available. He approached Ainsley Hall because he felt that the Hall mansion was the most suitable home for his family. The legend says that Hampton approached Hall and found him unwilling to part with his fabulous home. Hampton made various offers and Hall continued to decline the offers. When Hall hinted that he might accept $35,000, a king's ransom for the times, Hampton agreed to the price. To Hall's dismay, Hampton insisted on moving in immediately. He dispatched wagons and workers from his plantation. The Halls were moved out the next day.

Hall then purchased the land across the road on Walnut Street, a town square of 4 acres. He laid the foundation for a three-story house and retained Robert Mills to design it to be the most stately and magnificent home in Columbia. Just as the interior was completed, Hall died. His wife Sarah rejoined the Goodwyn family rather than complete the home. The Hall store on Richardson Street was sold and became the Rich Hotel.

Sarah Hall sold the mansion to the Theological Seminary of the Presbyterian Synod of South Carolina and Georgia at the request of Abram Blanding. They constructed dormitories, stables, a carriage house, and other dependencies for the use of the school. Classes began in 1831. Dr. George Howe came to Columbia and taught for 52 years. He influenced the curriculum and became the historian of the Presbyterian Church in South Carolina. Dr. Joseph R. Wilson, President Woodrow Wilson's father, and his uncle, James Woodrow, were faculty members during the Civil War.

The education of children was an early priority. The Free School Act was passed in 1811 and set aside plans for schools for females and males. It was called "free," however students were required to pay tuition of $25 per year, which covered 12 months of classes. Buildings were constructed for males in 1816 between Blanding and Laurel Streets. Students were taken to a campus in the sandhills during the summer, when the city was thought to be unhealthy. Wade Hampton II was one of the first students at the academy. His family's approval was an endorsement that attracted the children of other wealthy families.

The Columbia Female Academy was constructed a year later when funds from the sale of escheated property were turned over to the trustees. Dr. Elias Marks, the first principal, operated it for day students and boarding students. The tuition varied from $24 to $48 per year, depending upon the number of courses a young lady pursued. The boarding students paid as much as $200 per year. In 1829, the *Columbia Telescope* newspaper announced that classical studies were offered, including music, drawing, and painting on velvet. Marks left to open a private school in 1828; however, the school survived until the late 1800s.

The new capital needed a boost with public buildings and transportation. It was far from Charleston and also from the towns in the back-country. In 1816, there were 250 homes and 1,000 citizens. Taxes were set at 12¢ per $100 of property. Those who wanted to be exempt from patrol duty could pay an additional 5¢ per $100 and be excused. Those who wished to avoid working on the streets were taxed $2. Additional taxes were collected for personal property. A carriage cost $5 and $3 was charged for a wagon.

The Columbia Female Academy was established by an act of the legislature in 1811. Classes were held in the above facility until 1881 when it became a high school. The building was not razed until 1915, when Columbia High School was erected on the property.

Citizens were expected to help extinguish fires and every home was required to have a bucket for each chimney.

Stores stretched up Main and Gervais Streets. There were five fire brigades and every male citizen was expected to serve when needed. A new town hall was constructed north of the State House on Main Street. There was a market on the ground floor and offices and an auditorium on the second floor. A clock tower with a bell rose above the second story. It was a "large and good town clock . . . with bells sufficiently large to be heard throughout the town." The tower was built over the sidewalk and pedestrians walked through arches that served as an entrance to the street level market. Citizens arrived early to insure the best cuts of meat before the butcher left the market at 9 a.m. to sell his remaining cuts from his wagon as he drove through the streets of town. Those who missed the butcher traveled to the north end of Main Street to an area known as "butcher town."

A watchman was posted in the bell tower to look out for fires. He went on duty at dark. A second man arrived for duty at midnight; however, the first man was required to stay until daylight to assist in ringing the bell if a fire occurred. The bell was struck on the hour and half-hour and then the watchman would call out, "all's well!" throughout the night.

The same year, Governor David Williams urged the legislature to begin internal improvements in the state. When John Wilson was appointed as the state civil and military engineer, he requested $1 million for the construction of roads and canals. The legislature appropriated $1.9 million, and in 1819, a Board of Public Works was created. Wilson was made commissioner and Abram Blanding returned to Columbia to serve as the superintendent of the Board of Public Works. Blanding was aware that the citizens relied on wells for their water. In 1820, he personally financed the $75,000 cost to build a waterworks for the town. Water was pumped from a spring up to a wooden tank on Taylor's Hill using a Watt-type steam engine. The water then flowed by gravity to homes and businesses through cast iron and lead pipes. The project did not turn out to be profitable, so Blanding sold it to the city in 1835 for $25,000. A short time later, Walnut Street was renamed Blanding Street as a tribute to his farsightedness.

In 1820, Robert Mills was named engineer and architect for the Board of Public Works. After his appointment, he moved to Columbia from Charleston. He and Abram Blanding shared a mutual interest to make the rivers more navigable. They wanted to create a direct route between the up-country and Charles Town. Mills was the first American-educated architect. He worked with Henry Latrobe and James Hoban. Both Hoban and Latrobe were American architects who were educated in Europe. Mills was a frequent guest of Thomas Jefferson and lived at Monticello for two years. His visions of roads criss-crossing the state and river canals from Columbia to the coast made the town ahead of its time. He believed in improved roads and the canals as alternative routes and means of transportation.

From its earliest days, Columbia was known for its excellent soil and fertile farmland. The financial stability and success of the area depended on the ease of transporting cotton, tobacco, and other produce to market. There was a need for an additional mode of transportation to compete with land transportation between Charleston and the up-country. The potential of the waterways could not be overlooked. The construction of canals and locks were the initial projects of the state's newly founded Department of Public Works.

Wade Hampton I purchased this house from Ainsley Hall to use as a town house. In 1833 it was the finest home in Columbia. Hall immediately purchased the land across the street to build his new house. (Photo by Burke Salsi.)

One of their projects was the construction of the Columbia Canal. Work began on the project in 1815. The 22-mile canal was constructed flush with the left bank of the Saluda River and was designed to flow parallel to the Broad and Congaree Rivers. Flood gates and locks were erected on the canal to stabilize the water and protect freight boats from the dangerous rocks and thus help the boats traverse the rapids and falls. Four locks raised and lowered boats 36 feet. Two of the locks were formed after granite was blasted from the waterway and then used to construct the locks. The other two locks were built of brick. When Robert Mills arrived in Columbia in 1820, he was much in favor of the canal construction. He wrote in his *Statistics of South Carolina*:

> The great falls of the Congaree River begin at the upper end of the town, and terminate a little below the lower end; the pitch is 36 feet. To enable boats to overcome this obstruction, a canal and 4 locks are constructed. . . . They are of considerable importance to the country trade, as well as to that of Columbia. These locks are the largest in the State, being 16 feet wide and 100 feet long in their chamber with a lift of each about 9 feet. The largest bay boats are now able to ascend into the town.

The success of the new method of transportation was in direct relationship to the great positive economic development impact that it had on the town. By the use of small canal boats and steamboats, it was easier to transport cotton to Charleston. The boats could also return with freight. In 1827, 45,612 bales of cotton were shipped through the Columbia Canal. Robert Mills remarked:

> Columbia has engrossed much of the trade which King Street in Charleston formerly enjoyed; the produce of the back country stopping here to be transported by water to that city, instead of proceeding, as formally, by land. Several of the King Street merchants have removed to, or established houses in Columbia. Groceries and dry goods are now purchased as reasonable terms as in Charleston.

It took flat boats 24 days to make a round trip. The expense of these trips was often prohibitive because of the tolls. The charge was usually $1 per bale of cotton. Overland carts pulled by horses or mules took even longer and the fee was as much as $3 per bale. Two steamboats worked out of Columbia and proved to be more efficient by making the trip in less than ten days.

The boat lines running to Columbia played a very important part in the development of regular businesses in the town. The boats docked and the goods were off-loaded and hauled by horse-drawn drays into town. Cotton was then shipped as return cargo. Another line ran further up country and brought cotton and other products into Columbia. The boats ran to the foot of Boundary Street (now Elmwood Avenue). In 1833, 33,000 bales of cotton were

Abram Blanding and Robert Mills were ahead of their time when they designed many internal improvements for the new town of Columbia beginning in 1824. The Columbia Canal is pictured here c. 1905.

transported via the canal, and in 1840, a Broad River extension was added. During the Civil War, the Confederacy controlled the canal, which helped in the transport of supplies back and forth from the back-country though the Midlands to the low-country.

The construction of roads paralleled the development of the canals, if for no other reason than to get the legislators into town and back home again. Stagecoaches became the most popular vehicles for traveling. The existing Indian paths were widened and soon became dirt roads radiating in every direction from the center of Columbia. By 1826, the town was criss-crossed by ten roads that led in and out of town. The roads included the Barnwell Road a few miles south of town. The western road went to Augusta, Georgia through Lexington and Edgefield. The River Road led to Newberry, 45 miles northwest, and another route led to Winnsboro and Chester north of town. There were additional roads east to Stateburg and southeast to Camden.

Major internal improvements included a state road that was to join Charleston with the western counties by way of Columbia and the Orangeburg District. Parts of the road were leased to citizens who collected tolls and in return kept their section in good repair. In 1829, the segment from Charleston to Columbia was completed. There were eight toll stops between Columbia and Charleston. The expense of using the road kept down the usage. Citizens preferred to use the free by-ways in order to avoid paying.

The original plan for the state road included an eventual route all the way to Tennessee. It had to pass through North Carolina, and South Carolina had to have the cooperation of the other state. Although there would be no expense to North Carolina other than assistance in securing land, the state objected because it would not bring enough profit. The project was dropped. In 1825, bridges, roads, and states' rights were the principal debates. Attempts were made to erect a bridge over the Congaree. Even though the first structures proved to be temporary, the need for a sturdy permanent structure did not diminish. Meanwhile, the ferry remained the only reliable method of crossing the river.

Travel by horse and wagon and stagecoach was difficult. Road conditions were considered more or less treacherous depending upon weather conditions. Rain brought mud holes and afterward left deep ruts and corduroy patches. Crossing the deep sandhills in the summer heat was slow and hot. There were also swamps, streams, and rivers to traverse. When Bernhard, Duke of Saxe-Weimir Eisenach visited Columbia in December 1825, he recorded that Friday's Ferry located 3 miles below town was a "wretched boat." His visit and his impressions stirred politicians to take a look at the problem.

At the time, plans were already underway. The first substantial bridge across the Congaree River was a toll bridge built by William Briggs. It was completed in 1827 and connected Gervais Street west of the State House with the village of New Brookland. It was constructed with a steel frame and a wood plank roadbed, and was supported by 14 piers and abutments of solid granite. It was raised 28 feet above the river. A roof was constructed to protect the floor timbers from weather. The construction was made possible through the sale of shares totaling $75,000. A legislative act was passed authorizing the construction and it was completed in 1829. Floods threatened both bridges many times. However, they held up throughout the Civil War.

Early strides were made in public health. In the early 1820s, a board of health was organized to make a weekly return of the deaths that occurred in town. It was used to show

Cotton Town was established on Boundary Street (Elmwood Avenue), on the edge of town, in the early 1800s. Cotton was hauled from the river docks by horse and wagon. This photo was taken c. 1890.

comparative health with other towns. Even though this service did little to help improve the average citizen's day to day health, Robert Mills pronounced "there is no country more healthy than Columbia." He stated, "The summers are exempt from bilious, and the winters from inflammatory diseases." He was therefore in favor of the construction of a mental hospital. It was known at that time as the lunatic asylum and was the fourth built in the United States.

In 1822, Robert Mills designed the central building of brick with a large handsome portico supported by six columns. It was built to house 120 patients and was made as fire proof as possible. The massive facility was erected with substantial building materials using modern construction methods. Mills wrote:

> The design is both novel and convenient. It combines elegance with permanence, economy, and security from fire. The rooms are vaulted with brick, and the roof covered with copper. The building is large . . . with spacious corridors, hospital refectories, a medical hall, several parlours, keeper's apartments, kitchens, and sundry offices. The cost of the whole is considerable within $100,000.

As the state architect, Mills designed public works throughout South Carolina. However, Columbia was a new town and with it Mills set the style with large structures that dominated the landscape.

Despite the philanthropy behind the establishment of the asylum, it proved to be a financial drain on the state. The following notice appeared in the *Columbia Telescope* on June 15, 1832:

> By the act of the legislature, each Board of Commissioners of the poor, and each

40

city and town, are required to send their pauper idiots and lunatic epileptics to the lunatic asylum and support them there at the expense of the district, parish, city, or towns, charged with their support.

By the same act, all pauper patients now in the institution, or hereafter admitted are charged one hundred dollars per annum.

This regulation commenced on 17th of Dec. 1831. Pay patients will be received at 150 dollars per annum. The sum includes boarding, lodging, washing, servants, firewood, and medical attendance. Pay patients form a class by themselves. A larger sum will be demanded if more than ordinary care, comforts, or attendance are required.

In 1825, Mills published the *Atlas of South Carolina* and in 1826, the *Statistics of South Carolina.* They provided a status of the state at the time and a valuable window to the past for historians. The South Carolina Legislature ended the appropriations for the statewide building program in 1830. Mills moved to Washington, D.C. and accepted the position of federal architect. Among his designs are the U.S. Treasury Building and the Washington Monument. He also designed structures in Baltimore, Philadelphia, and Richmond.

Dr. Josiah Clark Nott and Dr. Robert W. Gibbes established a Preparatory School of Medicine in 1833. They lectured their students in a time when many doctors were trained by "reading" with established physicians. Nott delivered lectures on anatomy and surgery, while Gibbes spoke on chemistry. Gibbes became a noted college professor, doctor, newspaperman, and chemist. Nott published a notice in the *Columbia Telescope* on November 27, 1832: "Dr. J. Nott has opened an office on the Main Street one door above the State Bank and offers his services to the inhabitants of Columbia." The following January, Dr. Gibbes posted a notice in the same paper concerning public health: "The genuine chloride of lime prepared by Dr. Gibbes at the request of the town council can be obtained at cost by applying to the town marshal."

Gibbes was well known for giving medicine that smelled like rotten eggs for whooping cough. Children with a sore throat would have it examined by having the handle of a spoon put down their throats for the examination. The lancing of boils was a memorable experience, as was any serious illness or surgery. There were published homemade cures for most ailments. Those suffering from typhoid were never given anything but sweet milk. It was believed that if the patient was given sour milk or buttermilk, it would mean sure death.

Elias Marks resigned as principal of the Columbia Female Academy in 1827 to establish a school for women to honor his wife, Jane Barham Marks, who died the year before. The South Carolina Female Institute was constructed outside of the city limits in a place deemed healthier than the town and also because it was away from young men. Marks named the area Barhamville and the school was also often locally referred to as the Barhamville School.

Admission was opened to young ladies from the finest families in America. Theodore Roosevelt's mother, Martha Bulloch, was a student, as was John C. Calhoun's daughter, Anna Maria. The atmosphere was strict and exclusive. The curriculum was based on European schools. Students were well attended. They had servants to draw their tub baths and tend their fires. They were also allowed the indulgence of studying by candlelight in the evenings. The girls were not allowed to leave the campus alone and were restricted to walks on the school grounds. They were required to have written permission from their parents before they were allowed to converse with young gentlemen.

Nell Graydon, author of *Tales of Columbia,* related that the young men of South Carolina College enjoyed playing pranks at the school. They particularly enjoyed jumping the fence on Saturdays: "The gates were kept locked, but the students lifted their buggies over the fence and forced their horses to jump after them. At such times of crisis, the girls were ordered to close their blinds and stay in their rooms."

Dr. Marks retired in 1861 and moved to Washington, D.C. Two teachers, Madam Togno and Madam Sosnowski, kept the school going during the war. In 1869, the main building was destroyed by fire and afterwards the other structures were sold.

As larger plantations were created, planters were subject to the law of supply and demand. The price of cotton on the world market kept Columbia and the rest of the state developing agriculturally. However, during the War of 1812, the British, who had been large consumers of cotton, began buying in India. This caused the American price to drop to $14.33 per pound. Planters were strained financially. When banks called in loans, a depression ensued. Rains in the up-country caused valuable topsoil to wash away. Without income, many families emigrated to other states looking for new farmland. Many entire communities, especially in the up-country, moved together. Those who stayed found that trade declined. With fewer products to ship, the canals fell idle.

By 1820, the northern states were well ahead of the south in industrialization. While the southern farmers planted more and more acres of cash crops, the short growing season above the Mason-Dixon line proved to be the right environment for mills. As the north built great cities, people sought jobs that paid higher wages. The south stayed stuck in the old ways of clearing land, planting crops, and harvesting mostly by hand. The greater concentration of population in the growing cities consistently assured the north a majority and thus, greater power in Congress. It was during the 1820s that tariffs began to burden southern farmers and planters.

When Reverend Maxcy died in 1820, Dr. Thomas Cooper was named president of the South Carolina College. Cooper brought geology and political economy to the school. However, by 1835, he had anti-religious leanings that alarmed many of the school's biggest supporters. His political stance in favor of nullification brought the college into conflict. The state legislature demanded that the college reorganize and Cooper resigned.

A new president arrived at the South Carolina College in 1835. R.W. Barnwell put forth a great deal of effort in rebuilding the school and gaining the confidence of the legislature. He oversaw the construction of the South Carolina Library in 1840. Designed by Robert Mills, it was the first free-standing library structure in the country. Mills modeled the reading room after Bulfinch's plans for the original Library of Congress. In 1927, fireproof wings were added and in 1940 the library became known as the South Caroliniana Library.

President Barnwell also attempted to curtail the high spirits and pranks of the students by erecting a wall around the campus to aid in maintaining order. Students were involved in practical jokes targeted against professors and local citizens. They developed turkey stealing into a sport. Sometimes they de-feathered a bird and returned it "naked." Once they painted the college president's horse and shaved its tail. They often serenaded unpopular

Dr. Elias Marks established the South Carolina Female Institute outside of Columbia. He named the area Barhamville in honor of his wife and the school also became known as the Barhamville Academy.

professors by beating pots and pans at midnight and enjoyed chasing a calf around campus after tying a burning camphene ball to its tail.

In February 1856, South Carolina College students nearly landed in jail. Edward Niles got into a fight with the town marshal, John Burdell, and Niles ended up in the guardhouse. Niles's friends rushed back to the campus. Julian Selby reported being at work in the *South Carolinian* newspaper office and noticed more students than usual passing by. He was accustomed to seeing small groups cut through an open lot as they headed for Main Street where they promenaded most afternoons and evenings. He commented that they now "were gathering in force." Police Chief John Burdell rang an alarm bell, but despite his efforts the students scuffled with him, causing officers to draw their guns.

The students retreated and the police jumped to the conclusion that they were going back to the campus to procure guns, as all college students were required to participate in a military company. When they returned, many prominent citizens and professors had arrived to help calm the situation. Niles was released and the former college president, Reverend James H. Thornwell, defused the situation. After the students returned to the college, armed companies patrolled the streets all night. The cadet military unit was disbanded and students were no longer allowed to promenade on Main Street. Some students withdrew from the college.

Student pranks and confrontations with authority were thought to be a result of the administration's attempts to discipline privileged young men who were immersed socially in horse racing, gambling, card playing, and outdoor activities. While in Columbia, the constraints of remaining on a small campus to study, to attend classes, and to follow rules were often just too much to cope with.

3. The Town is Settled

Improvements to the roads brought improvements to stagecoach service. In 1825, regular service was established to Augusta, Camden, and Greenville. By 1840, coaches ran routes north, south, east, and west. Columbia attracted visitors from Charleston, Augusta, Charlotte, and Greensboro, North Carolina. And likewise, residents of Columbia enjoyed excursions out of the city. There was talk of extending a line to intersect with the great western route through Knoxville, Tennessee.

In 1833, many articles and advertisements were placed in the *Columbia Telescope* advertising services of hotels and taverns. The China Hotel in Stateburg ran the following:

> The subscriber informs his friends that he is ready to accommodate travellers and boarders. His table will be furnished with the best the market can produce. His stables will be plentifully provided with the best provender and attended by honest and careful hostlers. No expense will be spared to render those comfortable that may favor him with their patronage.

While hotels and taverns advertised for patrons, the stagecoach services were establishing rules. William J.M. Millan posted notices in the *Telescope* stating that he would not be responsible for loss or miscarriage of any trunks, boxes, packages, or articles of any description carried or sent in any of the coaches with or without passengers. "All goods are considered at risk of the owner or will not be taken."

As the stage pulled into town, it was often followed by several curious boys eager to see the occupants. They could judge by the appearance of the luggage the importance of the passengers. Julian Mood was among those boys. He recorded in the Mood family history how much he enjoyed watching the stage go by and listening for the driver's horn.

Even after the inauguration of passenger service on the river, many preferred to keep their feet on dry ground. Regardless, traveling was an adventure. Julian Selby wrote about a stagecoach trip with his mother to Charleston in February 1837 to attend "Race Week." He said, "Some went by steamboat from Granby down the Congaree to the Santee and then through the Santee Canal to the Cooper River and to the City by the Sea." Selby and his mother chose to take the stagecoach to Branchville and then by steam cars into Charleston.

During the return trip, they traveled through an area known as Hogbrook Swamp, which was nearly impassable due to a rain storm. One of the male passengers Selby dubbed "an out and out Yankee" asked to walk and after a while he got ahead of the stage. In the meantime, the stage nearly overturned during an attempt to pass through the mire. The interior oil lamps were extinguished and the lady passengers found it difficult to find their shoes before they were safely pulled from the coach. It took a long time to get the stagecoach in service and the walker was found waiting beside the road. He immediately inquired about the ladies. They were pleased that he had manners to ask about their health before asking about the condition of his personal belongings. Selby continued:

> The name of the driver was Happy Jack. He was a hearty good-natured soul. He and his wife had a comfortable home near Sandy Run. The road passed within a mile of his house, but a turn required two miles to reach it. His wife prepared coffee, biscuits, meat. She banked the fire in the big stone fireplace and retired. When Jack reached the nearest point, he would blow, "The White Cockade and the Black Cockade" or some other simple air on his horn, give a loud wind-up toot, and yell, "Elizabeth." This roused the passengers and woke up Elizabeth. By the time the stage arrived, a hot breakfast was on the table, much to the gratitude of the travelers and the pecuniary advantage of Elizabeth.

The mid 1820s brought new concerns for the economy. John C. Calhoun of South Carolina served as vice president of the United States under John Quincy Adams. There

Wheelers Transfer and Livery was only one of the establishments serving the traveling public c. 1880. Stagecoach service was available in Columbia through the nineteenth century.

was a depression following the War of 1812 and citizens were hostile against the Bank of the United States. Northern textile producers requested that Congress raise the tariff on cotton and woolen fabric imported from Europe. They felt that the cheaper cloth from overseas was hurting their businesses. South Carolina was caught in the middle, because the state exported tons of raw cotton to mills abroad. The southern farmers knew that the European mill owners would pressure them to lower prices per pound. Despite strong opposition from the south, Congress passed the Tariff Act of 1824.

Then three years later, northern manufacturers asked for an additional tariff. A protest meeting was held in Columbia in July 1827. Delegates felt that the tariffs were equal to "taxation without representation." Thomas Cooper of the South Carolina College believed that Congress could regulate commerce for revenue, defense, and retaliation, but not for unequal protection that favored the manufacturers and burdened the agriculturalists. Cooper warned Congress that the future of the United States was at stake.

The South Carolina Legislature was urged to refuse to accept another federal tariff law. Calhoun suggested that it be rendered null and void—a type of suspension of a law just within the territory of the state. Despite overwhelming opposition, the act passed, causing the rate to increase by 50 percent. Cotton prices fell from 32¢ per pound to 13¢ per pound and the state's economy was nearly wrecked.

Senator Calhoun prepared a statement on behalf of South Carolina in 1828. He set forth his philosophy of "nullification." His idea was based on the doctrine of states' rights, the concept that each of the states had been sovereign and independent before the signing of the Constitution. He pointed out that the states had only been "united" for a generation. Calhoun felt if the tariff was not reduced, South Carolina might "interpose their sovereignty" to stop the application of the law.

John C. Calhoun served as a United States senator. He was a devout believer in Nullification and fought for state's rights for South Carolina until his death

When Jackson removed the government deposits from the Bank of the United States, Calhoun joined Daniel Webster and Henry Clay in the formation of the Democratic Whig Party to oppose the re-election of the President. They strongly felt that government should promote economic growth for all of its states. Calhoun failed to receive the presidential nomination and ran for vice president. Despite their best effort, Jackson was elected President and Calhoun was reelected vice president.

John Taylor served as governor between December 1826 and December 1828. He supported states' rights; however, he opposed the nationalism of Calhoun. He advocated using legal means to settle the tariff question and refused to call a special session of the legislature in 1828 to debate the issues. He was opposed to South Carolina acting without the support of the other Southern states.

From that time on, the citizens of the state heard about nullification, secessions, and slavery. In August of 1830, the *Southern Times and State Gazette* published articles urging nullification as the only means of relief. On September 20, 1830, a states' rights meeting was held to organize a States' Rights and Free Trade Party. By July 18, associations were organized throughout the state. Years of anger, discussion, debate, and oration ensued. Duels were almost a daily occurrence in Columbia, as well as elsewhere in the state.

Nullification loomed larger and larger and was a topic of debate from the living room to the legislature. The *Columbia Telescope* of June 5, 1832 covered a public festival given to honor Governor Hamilton. The public toast recognized the governor "for generously devoting himself to the defence of Southern Rights and is qualified for every crisis. And southern people will support him in the great cause, in every peril and at every hazard."

Governor Hamilton called for an extra legislative session that met on November 19, 1832. Southerners sought to effect equal treatment by the United States Legislature with the passage of the Ordinance of Nullification on November 24, 1832. The document accused the Congress of the United States of the:

> giving of bounties to classes and individuals engaged in particular employments, at the expense and to the injury and oppression of other classes and individuals, and by wholly exempting from taxation certain foreign commodities, such as not produced or manufactured in the United States, to afford a pretext for imposing higher and excessive duties on articles similar to those intended to be protected. . . . and violated the true meaning and intent of the constitution, which provided for equality in imposing the burdens of taxation upon the several States and portions of the confederacy.

The Union Party then met December 22. On January 3, 1833, the *Columbia Telescope* published an "Extra Edition" containing the entire address of the party's December Convention. The January 29 edition published Governor Robert Y. Hayne's proclamation:

> to observe Thursday, January 31, 1833 as a day of solemn fasting, humiliation and prayer imploring the almighty to bestow his blessings upon the proceedings of this body that they may eventuate in the promotion of his glory and in restoring and perpetuating the liberty and prosperity of our native state.

On the day the nullification order was to be effected, it was suspended awaiting Congress to pass the Clay Tariff Compromise of 1833. It ultimately stopped the nullification proceedings, yet the bitterness did not die. The tariff was lowered, but it was not low enough. Farmers bore the burden with anger and frustration while the north continued to control Congress. Balls, barbeques, parades, and commencements were the great events. Politicians attended events for the opportunity of making a stump speech to instruct citizens as to the proper way to construe the constitution and the true philosophy of states' rights.

The state prepared for a possible war. The sum of $200,000 was appropriated for purchasing arms at the Citadel. The militia was called out for regular drills and money was appropriated for building a magazine. Between 1840 and 1860, Columbia was known for its military as much as for its markets. The monthly muster was one of the chief entertainments and well drilled troops created a spectacle on the streets that thrilled on-lookers.

Julian Selby talked about the militia of the day:

> The old militia law in South Carolina was stringent. Every male individual between the ages of 18 and 50 was compelled to do military duty, either in uniformed companies or the "Beats" as those God-forsaken looking soldiers used to be called. The consequence was Columbia had seven uniformed companies: The Richland Rifles, Governor's Guards, Carolina Blues, Emmett Guards, Greys, Flying Artillery, Richland Light Dragoons, and on regimental or battalion parades, College Cadets and Cedar Creek Rifles. Fourth of July was one of the regular parade days. The companies would assemble at 6 o'clock in the morning to march to Taylor's Hill, the Artillery fired a salute, and they marched down again, had a collation, and dismissed for the day.

Those who didn't have a gun used sticks. The military exhibition was over by 9 a.m. The afternoon of the Fourth featured a parade of men in costumes followed by an evening fireworks display.

A prolonged depression began in 1837; banks collapsed in 1839. This did not discourage the dyed in the wool politicians who favored nullification. Farmers suffered the most; tariffs destroyed the value of cotton, wheat went down to 10¢ a bushel, and corn was given away. The farmers got no relief until a preemption bill was passed in 1842.

William Gilmore Simms, author, plantation owner, and attorney, was an outspoken unionist and worked to keep the union together. He was elected to serve in the legislature from 1844–1846. His pleas mostly fell on deaf ears. Up until secession in 1860, nullification was one of the most notable political events in the history of South Carolina.

The Presidential campaign of 1841 elicited much debate and excitement. The Whigs were in the majority and held meetings where speakers had to yell to the crowds to be heard. The former sheriff, Jesse DeBruhl, led the Democrats. They wore red caps, paraded the streets, and used the circus building for their headquarters. There was much "mud-slinging" and the young people joined in by yelling such expressions as "Whigs eat dead pigs" and "Democrats eat dead rats."

Duels between gentlemen continued as the preferred manner of settling issues. Many men favored the code duello as a method of improving morals and manners. Louis Wigfall

25/Volunteer rifle company at Hyatt Park off North Main Street.

Columbia was a military town where all the militia units drilled regularly. The volunteer rifle company is pictured in front of the Hyatt Park pavilion off North Main Street.

was considered to be the best shot in South Carolina. His duel in 1841 with Preston Brooks was his most famous. He was involved in several duels of honor prior to his marriage and suffered various wounds; however, none were mortal. Wigfall graduated from the South Carolina College in the late 1830s in a time when the students had been influenced for decades by staunch beliefs in the right of secession and the need of a strong state government supporting states' rights. Many graduates of the time developed a strong interest in politics. Wigfall and his friends were followers of John C. Calhoun. Many in his class went on to serve in the legislature and his close friend, John L. Manning, became governor.

By 1850, Columbia experienced prosperity because cotton was undeniably king. It was the state's biggest cash crop, and Columbia was a marketplace for cotton as well as other goods. The farms beyond the city limits produced mostly cotton and tobacco. Farmers from the up-country shipped their products into Columbia for transportation by train to Charleston where much of it was shipped abroad.

Several generations had put down roots in Columbia by 1856 and the city was a destination for political events, court day, markets, entertainment, and shopping. Julian Mood recalled that fire tournaments and gander pullings attracted crowds. Fire companies, especially the Independent and Palmetto, competed in categories for prizes.

It was decided that construction of a stately and larger State Capitol building was needed for more than one reason. The legislature wanted a fireproof building for the storage of state records. Plantation owners who had acquired homes in town wanted a vast new facility to create greater confidence in the local economy and to give an appearance of stability to the state government. A modern structure was envisioned to provide greater comfort for the members of the general assembly. The new building was begun in 1851. In the meantime, the town was granted a charter to become the City of Columbia in 1854. A mayor and six aldermen were elected annually to govern the new city.

A chief of police and nine patrolmen replaced the town guard and seven officers. Two policemen patrolled at all times in order to protect the residents and visitors, yet carried only sticks for weapons. Those who erred in judgment were taken to the guardhouse on Main Street near the Western Union office.

After three years of little progress on the State House by architect P.H. Hammarskold, Governor John L. Manning called in John R. Niernsee to act as a consultant. Niernsee found that inferior material was being used and Hammarskold was released from his contract. Niernsee recommended that the building be razed; after his design was selected, he moved from Baltimore to Columbia in 1854. His plan included an elaborate fireproof structure with an underground drainage system and beautiful landscaped grounds as a park for citizens. The legislature decided that there was not enough land available to build a proper structure because they wanted the new building located close to the center of the property. They voted to tear down Hammarskold's structure and purchased the adjacent block of property allowing plenty of room for the old State House during the construction of the new one.

Work began when the first stone was laid on April 21, 1855. Granite for the building came from local quarries, most of it from a quarry at Granby, on the west side of the river. The quarry was opened for the purpose of mining stone for the capitol.

The following was written in *Columbia: Capital City of South Carolina, 1786–1936*, edited by Helen Kohn Hennig:

> Columbia lies on the last outcrop of granite in the Santee drainage area. Strange as it may seem it was not until 1856 that any attempt was made to use this excellent building material. The State House is the first structure in the city made of this

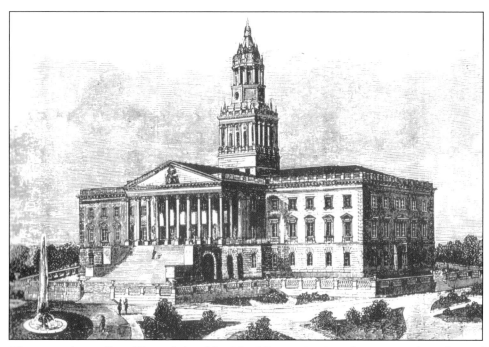

The proposed new State House designed by John Niernsee is pictured as a magnificent fireproof structure with an imposing tower.

stone. A quarry was opened on the river where Granby Lane ran down to the landing and where a ferry was once operated. The stone was of most excellent quality and the great monolithic columns on the front and back porches of the State House testify as to its fine grain and beauty.

In order to carry the stone from the quarry to the site of the building a tram road was built which ran down Main Street to the corner of College Street and thence to the west through the woods and through the present Olympia Village to the quarry. The immense stones, weighing tons, were put on the trams and hauled up the hill by oxen to the building and there squared, dressed, and carved.

There seem to have been no native-born stone masons, for the stone cutters were all Irish or Americans from the north.

The Roman Catholics arrived from Ireland in 1821 to work on the canal and more Irishmen arrived in the 1850s to work on the new State House. St. Peter's Roman Catholic Church was established in 1824 and was located on Assembly Street between the local theater and the circus grounds. According to Julian Selby, locals referred to the location as "Christ between the thieves." The Catholics brought St. Mary's College to town in 1851; it catered to well to do young ladies who boarded. The Ursuline sisters built their convent in a three-story brick building on the corner of Main and Blanding Streets in 1856 where the James L. Tapp Department Store was constructed decades later.

Public transportation came to Columbia in 1822, when a street railway operated for the transportation of freight. It was pulled by mules and horses. It ran from Cotton Town at the intersection of Elmwood Avenue and Main Street through the middle of Main and Gervais Streets to the river where warehouses were located adjacent to the Columbia Canal. One of the horses was named "Old Drag" because he had a habit of sitting down in the middle of the road.

By 1840, Columbia was known as a pretty place. Trees and gardens punctuated its organized avenues. Though it had a reputation as a market center and "Cotton Town" was the trade area for cotton producers, most residents paid attention to the appearance of the town. Many families had a garden and the wealthy had elaborate homes with vast flower, fruit, and vegetable gardens. The Hampton House was known all over the South for its garden of rare species.

Sidney Park was established in the 1840s at the bottom of Taylor's Hill, now known as Arsenal Hill and the present site of Finlay Park. It was named after town warden Algernon Sidney Johnston, who wished to create a place of beauty on the low flat land at the bottom of the ravine. It became a show place. The *South Carolinian* newspaper of April 22, 1864 said, "One of the loveliest walks or rides in Columbia is Sidney Park and its vicinity, about the hour of 5 p.m. Nature is donning herself in her spring attire, the birds make music, the children prattle with their nurses, the young ladies enjoy flirtations with their gallants." The park stayed a part of the active life of Columbians until well after the Civil War.

In 1841, Columbia had its first extensive conflagration. Julian Selby was an eye-witness and described the fire in his *Memorabilia*:

> The flames broke out in a blacksmith shop in Davis' alley. It destroyed the entire
> Main Street front on the side of the square. It also wiped out the property from

Sidney Park was a lovely public park enjoyed by the citizens of Columbia. The park featured a pond with swans, trees, and flowers. The site was razed to make way for a Seaboard Railroad facility.

Plain to the two story buildings extending to the corner of Taylor, known as "Brick Range." The principal stores in town G.V. Antwerp, John I Gracey, A. Young, Alfred North, John McKenzie, Elias Pollock, I.D. Mordecai, Cohen and Bell, the South Carolinian Printing office and others. Wade Hampton and a sailor named Neville worked to save that property. The crowd cheered them. At the time, the fire department consisted of two small hand engines. They were the Independent (white) and the Vigilant (colored) with a so-called hook and ladder company (the principal occupation of the members of the latter being to keep mischievous boys from running away with the useless appendage whenever it was brought to a fire.) The members of the companies worked efficiently and prevented what was at first thought would be an extensive and destructive fire. Mr. Latta presented the white company with a silver-speaking trumpet and gave Mr. Galloway Monteith's colored boys a liberal "feed."

During the fire, Mrs. Alexander, the wife of a clothing merchant, saw that her two young children were in safe hands, and then proceeded to dress herself. She was notified several times that the building was on fire, and she must come out; but her sole reply was, "Not till I lace my corsets. I'm not going to catch my death of cold."

When the railroad came in the 1830s, there was a competition between the railroad and riverboat companies for passengers and trade. A regular steamboat service had begun in 1821 to carry passengers and cargo between Columbia and Charleston. The train service was viewed with great anticipation because a one-way trip to Charleston by river could take 10–12 days. The era of road building nearly ceased with the coming of the railroad. Towns throughout the state became connected by railroads rather than roads.

In October 1830, the first locomotive came to Charleston from New York by ship. It was named the *Best Friend of Charleston*. On Christmas Day 1830, 141 people were transported over 6 miles of track at 25 miles per hour. The race was on to connect South Carolina by rail. By 1833, 136 miles of track was laid to Hamburg, South Carolina. It became the longest railroad track in America. Branch lines were then laid to Columbia and Camden. By 1860, South Carolina had 1,000 miles of track. Columbia instantly became a marketing center.

A group in Columbia felt that it would be more practical to construct the road from Branchville, which was already on the Charleston line. The group formed the Columbia Railroad Company in December 1833. The second plan failed, even after the stockholders determined that the railroad to Columbia would be indispensable to the growth and land values of the area. Finally, in 1837, the Louisville, Cincinnati, and Charleston Railroad Company bought the stock. Their original plan was to build a line that would link Charleston and Cincinnati, Ohio. By September 1839, the contracts were let for preparing the roadbed. The project met with delays caused by bad weather and lack of funding, yet passenger service was finally opened to Columbia on June 20, 1842.

Rail rates concerned the earliest passengers and freight shippers. In 1838, even before the railroad came to Columbia, the legislators took over the duty of setting rates. The first rate was set at 7.5¢ per mile for passengers. The June issue of *The Farmer and Planter* noted that it cost $1.25 to transport a 75¢ sack of salt from Charleston to Laurens. As more train tracks converged on Columbia, rates of the various lines became competitive.

The mayor of Charleston attended the official celebration on June 28 and arrived on the first train. There was drinking and feasting, and toasts were offered by the great men of the day, including the mayor of Charleston and Wade Hampton. Wade Hampton offered his praise to the city of Charleston. William Myers, intendent of Columbia, offered, "What man has magnificently joined together, surely God will protect against the ravage of time and the wars of the elements."

Julian Selby recalled seeing the first train as it reached Columbia:

> There was a big time in the capital city on the arrival of the first train. The Washington Light Infantry and French Artillery came from Charleston besides a number of civilians, to participate in the festivities. There was a barbeque on the lot adjacent to the depot, with plenty of spiritual accompaniments—great tubs filled with punch and lemonade, were scattered around promiscuously—lager beer was not in vogue then. Ice was something rare, except when winter reigned. My good friend, Charles Neuffer, the genial German, superintended the fluid distribution and gave me several lemons, sufficient sugar and a big lump of ice, to take home and prepare a lemonade for my mother.
>
> Mr. Henry T. Peake, afterward Superintendent of the South Carolina Railroad, was one of the first engineers with the "Ravenel." According to my recollections, the "Robert Y. Hayne," a diminutive locomotive, hauled the first train. Every afternoon crowds of people would go down to see the train arrive from Charleston, the run required 12 hours. The remark of an Irishman, who had stationed himself at a respectable distance from the locomotive, impressed me,[sic] He said, "If that ain't hell in a harness, what is it?"

All in all, the railroad was the miracle that opened inaccessible rural areas and connected them to markets. Despite the small engines, the narrow rickety tracks, and the barrel-shaped passenger cars that had a tendency to roll downhill when jarred, the railroad succeeded. J.F. Williams noted that sometimes the rail would come loose at the end and would turn up and run through the floor of the cars. These were called "snake heads" and were dreaded by the engineers. The connection to Camden was completed in October of 1848. In 1853, the road was complete through Marion and Florence to Wilmington, North Carolina. The railroad arrived in Greenville in 1854 and was completed all the way to Walhalla in 1857. The Charlotte and South Carolina Railroad Company planned a road to connect Camden and Charlotte. When the greatest percentage of stock subscriptions was purchased by Columbians, the route was changed to connect Charlotte and Columbia.

The General Assembly again passed the 1850 Act to Provide for the Defense of the State. An amount of $350,000 was appropriated for the military including munitions and coastal defense. The Richland Light Dragoons and the Flying Artillery Company of the Dragoons rearmed and increased their training regimen. William Glaze and his partner Thomas Radcliffe of Glaze and Radcliffe in the "Brick Range" received orders for armaments. They provided over 274 rifles and 100 muskets. These affairs led Glaze to partner with Benjamin Flagg and James Boatwright to organize the Palmetto Armory on the corner of Laurel and Lincoln Streets. Boatwright had political and banking connections and Flagg was experienced in arms production. He was recruited to come to Columbia after the Act of 1850 was ratified.

During this period, Celia Mann, a Charleston slave, worked as a midwife and purchased her freedom. She walked all the way to Columbia where she continued her work and lived as a free citizen. She purchased a cottage at 1403 Richland Street and lived there with her husband and four daughters. Her home was spared in the 1865 fire and remained in the family until 1970. She was a founding member of the First Calvary Baptist Church that met in her basement. Her family members worked as bakers, tailors, and musicians. They carried forth an entrepreneurial spirit during the post war years.

Celia's second husband, Bill Simons, was a member of the Joe Randall Band. In *Old and New Columbia*, J.F. Williams recalled that Joe Randall was a bandmaster and taught bands all over the country. He said, "There was no white band here and the Negro bands turned out for all ocassions."

There was much excitement and speculation until the secessionists were defeated in 1851. Then the Convention of the People of South Carolina was held in April 1852. The voting body lost interest in the cause of secession; however, the convention members adopted a resolution stating that the state of South Carolina had a right to secede. Following the convention, the thought of war waned and the militia lost enthusiasm. The Palmetto Armory became the Palmetto Iron Works. Glaze and his partners turned their attention toward the manufacture of steam engines, boilers, cotton gins, farm implements, and sugar mills.

As the north moved forward, in many ways South Carolina lagged behind. Columbia continued doing things the old way. Disagreements between the well-to-do politicians of the old guard and the new guard who were mostly sons and close relations escalated. The old gentry quelled the ideas of the newly educated young men by appointing friends and

Celia Mann walked from Charleston to Columbia to start a life of freedom. She worked as a midwife and was a member of the First Calvary Baptist Church, which was organized in the basement of her house. (Photo by Burke Salsi.)

kin to the highest positions in government. The old politicians prevailed, at least until the end of the War Between the States.

In his diary, James H. Hammond stated that the government "became that of an autocracy when a colony of old families ruled the legislature." In the antebellum period, the General Assembly elected the governor and the U.S. senators. A famous letter in the South Caroliniana Library written by an anonymous author states, "We have just passed through an exciting election in which Mr. Preston having the most money has come out victorious."

The legislature considered establishing a military school in the early days of the nullification debates. Its creation may have also been a result of young men from the Richland Volunteer Rifles serving in Florida in February of 1863 in a campaign to subdue the Seminole Indians. The Arsenal Academy in Columbia and the Citadel Academy in Charleston were created by the same act on December 20, 1842. Both schools provided young men with military training, as well as an education. Appropriations were made to accommodate scholarship students along with paying students. The Arsenal Academy was located on Taylor's Hill near the arsenal. The original rectangular two-story buildings were joined by a "main" three-story structure in 1852, creating a grand appearance. In 1855, brick officers' quarters were constructed away from the old buildings in front and to the side.

There were plenty of small private schools, tutoring, and exclusive places to study in Columbia. Those who could afford an elite education could pick and choose where they wished to study. The *Daily Telegraph* of October 19, 1847 listed 13 schools in the area and these did not include the ones that privately tutored and held sessions for a few students.

There were also free schools that most people avoided unless there was no other alternative. The Odd Fellows established the Palmetto Lodge School in 1844 and charged a much lower tuition than the academies and seminaries. James Carlisle, who later became president of Wofford College, was the first president. When the school could not provide suitable student housing, the legislature stepped in and donated a lot. A group of ladies staged a charity fair and raised $1,000 to help construct a new building. It opened in 1850 on Lincoln Street and E.E. Bellinger became the principal when Carlisle went to the Male Academy. In 1856, Henry Purcell's School on Washington Street at the rear of Perry's Meat Market merged with the Odd Fellows School. J.F. Williams was a student at Purcell's and related a good story from his school days in *Old and New Columbia*:

> There was a warehouse near the school with whiskey stored in it. Boys found it and crawled under the floor and with gimlets bored through into the barrel and soon had all they wanted. The Negroes working in the shop got their dinner buckets and filled them. Soon they were all drunk. The boys who did the boring

The first library at the South Carolina College is known as the South Caroliniana Library and is still standing on the horseshoe. It was designed by Robert Mills and constructed as the only free standing library in the United States in 1840. (Photo by Burke Salsi.)

and the Negroes were taken to the guardhouse and whipped.

John C. Calhoun became a champion of his state. He served as a window to the other world in the north. He interpreted an intellectual justification of where southerners believed their economy rested. He opposed all attempts at restoring a tariff and spent many years promoting southern unity. While serving as U.S. secretary of state, he supported the annexation of Texas as a way of opening the area to slavery and helping to establish a sectional balance.

Calhoun believed that each section should have a veto on the actions of the federal government. Until the end, he opposed the Compromise of 1850. Three days before his death, Calhoun was too weak to deliver the 42-page speech that he wrote against northern aggression and continued conciliation; Senator James Murray Mason read it to Congress. He recommended that two separate nations be formed if differences could not be settled. He felt the two sections should agree to part amicably. He was one of the catalysts for the establishment of the Confederacy and the passage of secession, but he would never have wished for war. Calhoun died on March 31, 1850, ten years before secession. His funeral in Charleston was the most elaborate the state had ever seen.

Julian Selby reported that the last use of the old theatre on Assembly Street was a moving representation of the funeral of Senator Calhoun as he was taken from Washington, D.C. to Charleston for burial. It depicted the arrival of the steamer *Governor Dudley* from Wilmington as it was escorted by the *Metamore* and other steam craft in port:

> It showed the procession and finally the interment of the body in the plot in the rear of the Circular Church on Church Street. Notwithstanding the solemnity of the subject, laughter was caused by the machinery not working properly. The soldiers would appear to take a rapid step or two and stop, then start, with similar movements by the horsemen and dragoons.

The 1830s and 1840s were a time of political identity, a completion of public works, the growth of Columbia as an important market town, the coming of the railroad, and the expansion of the population. The 1840s and 1850s saw a new generation take over in a manner resembling the old regime. It was a time when tallow candles were used, homemade shoes were worn, matches were a luxury for the well to do, and people named their sons States Rights. By 1856, Columbia had grown to over 6,000 and there was a new consciousness of developing the economy outside of the old plantation society and there was an interest in new ways of doing things. But in Columbia old ways died hard, grudges were not forgotten, and citizens could not get used to living through boom and bust economies.

The years of debates over nullification and secession had to be resolved. By 1860, it was apparent that the leaders of government had reached a breaking point. They were convinced that the north had reduced the south to political slavery. Palmetto cockades and tiny blue flags became common decorations for hats and clothing to show support for South Carolina. Most public gatherings outside of church meetings included politics and patriotism. Reverend Henry Mood's son long remembered the words to a popular song sung on such occasions:

> We are a band of brothers, and
> Native to the soil,
> Ready to fight for liberty we
> Won by honest toil.
> And when our rights are threatened,
> The cry comes near and far;
> Hurrah! For the bonny blue flag,
> That bears a single star!

The energy at political meetings during 1860 was charged with anticipation. Traditional celebrations took on a contagious, almost electrical atmosphere. E.J. Arthur was among those against war. Yet he hung on to the belief that the Yankees would not fight.

The Arsenal Academy was established by an act of the legislature in 1856 at the same time the Citadel Academy was established in Charleston. The school trained young men in scholarly pursuits and for military service. It accepted both paying and scholarship students.

4. THE CIVIL WAR

The talk of secession was over three decades old when the Secession Convention took place in 1860. Changing the way the state did business with other states and countries had long been a sore point between South Carolina and the United States Congress. South Carolina politicians were fed up with unfair taxes placed on farmers and unfair legislation that benefited the northern states. The clash of two different cultures with two entirely different ways of life and two different agendas created an additional schism. South Carolina wanted to withdraw from the Union as early as 1832 and run her business as a sovereign country.

There had never been a compromise in the U.S. Congress that favored South Carolina on any issue, no matter how strong the representation from the south. The formation of abolitionist groups and their stand on the subject of slavery caused everyone—citizen and politician alike—to feel there would be an inevitable conflict. The New England abolitionists represented everything that was wrong about the north telling the south what to do. For years, public meetings were held all over the state. Prominent orators held forth for hours speaking to large audiences on the subject of secession. The north–south situations infuriated Robert Barnwell Rhett, Milledge Bonham, John H. Means, James H. Adams, and Maxcy Gregg. They delivered many convincing orations in favor of secession.

On the other side, Robert Barnwell, Benjamin F. Perry, Wade Hampton III, and William Gilmore Simms urged restraint. There was a great deal at stake because by 1860, Columbia had reached prominence with a stable year-round population of 8,052. The economy, as well as the population, swelled with every session and convention of the legislature.

When Colonel Francis W. Pickens returned to South Carolina in 1860 following his service as the U.S. ambassador to Russia under President Buchanan, he found Columbians in favor of immediate secession. As the grandson of the Revolutionary War leader Andrew Pickens and the son of Governor Andrew Pickens, Jr., it was easy for him to reenter state politics despite his two year absence from the state.

On December 10, 1860, the legislature elected Pickens governor. Although he urged restraint, outgoing governor William Gist made a farewell speech urging secession: "The delay of the Convention for a single week to pass the Ordinance of Secession will have a blighting and chilling influence on other States." The legislature then chose December 17th as the day to decide on secession at a special convention to be held in Columbia.

The hotels quickly filled and private homes took in guests. Between the 10th and the 17th, there was a celebratory atmosphere. Banners and flags were hung all over town. A white banner with a lone star and green palmetto tree was raised over Glaze's foundry. The Methodist Women's College students made a blue silk banner with the motto *nunc aut Nunquam*—now or never—and hung it at their college on Plain Street.

The new brick First Baptist Church was selected as the site of the Secession Convention. The sanctuary was full and there was standing room only before noon on December 17. General David Flavel Jamison was elected president of the convention. Many fiery speeches were made urging immediate secession. Maxcy Gregg was one of the prominent Columbians who worked as an activist in the secession movement. He was a brilliant leader, an attorney, and a veteran of the Mexican War. He helped draft the Secession Ordinance. Dr. Joseph LeConte, professor of chemistry and geology at the South Carolina College, published his autobiography in 1903 and recorded: "The Secession Convention which sat in Columbia in December 1860, was the gravest, ablest, and most dignified body of men I ever saw brought together. They were fully aware of the gravity of their action."

In the afternoon, news of an outbreak of smallpox reached the convention. Delegates immediately left town to reconvene in Charleston. The governor, convention representatives, dignitaries, and other interested parties left for the railroad station in carriages and on horseback. The depot was enveloped in frantic confusion as crowds rushed the ticket windows. J.F. Williams wrote that smallpox affected a number of people

First Baptist Church on Hampton Street was the site of the first meeting of the Secession Convention in December 1860. The handsome brick sanctuary was erected in 1859 and replaced a wood-frame building. This photo was taken c. 1900.

in the city. Those who died were taken by a horse drawn cart to be buried at night. The burial carts were then left in the woods to rot.

The official vote in favor of secession was delivered in Charleston on December 20, 1860 and the Ordinance was signed. The news was joyously received throughout South Carolina. The demonstrations in Columbia were boisterous. Canons were fired, bells were rung, and rosin barrels were set on fire in the middle of Main Street. Minutemen organized and were ready to deploy in a moment's notice. From that point, the convention and not the legislature governed the state until it joined the Confederacy. The new governor had the power to organize the militia and enlist volunteer troops. States Rights Gist was appointed inspector general of South Carolina.

Convention members later felt that Governor Pickens was overstepping his authority. A five-member Executive Council, including the governor, took over the responsibilities of conducting war. In December 1862, when Milledge L. Bonham became governor, the legislature abolished the council and took control of the state government.

When secession was announced, many of the students of The South Carolina College enlisted in the army. Joseph LeConte recorded in his autobiography that the college classes continued for a while with diminished numbers. However, in June of 1862 after the Seven Days Battle for Richmond, the remaining students volunteered. Studies were suspended until the end of the war and college buildings were used as a hospital. The Arsenal Academy and the Citadel Academy were united as The South Carolina Military Academy on January 28, 1861; both students and officers were formed into a local public guard.

On February 4, 1861, representatives from Alabama, Georgia, Florida, Louisiana, Mississippi, South Carolina, and Texas met in Montgomery, Alabama to form a government. Four days later, the Confederate States of America was formed and began setting up a provisional congress. Jefferson Davis defeated Robert Rhett of South Carolina to become president. The Confederate Constitution was approved on March 1 and three envoys traveled to Washington, D.C. to negotiate a peaceful split.

Major Robert Anderson moved his company of U.S. troops from Fort Moultrie to Fort Sumter in Charleston. Governor Francis Pickens retaliated by taking Castle Pinckney in Charleston Harbor. Two weeks later, the *Star of the West* was sent to supply Fort Sumter, but she retreated when fired on by South Carolina troops. General Pierre Beauregard ordered the bombardment of Fort Sumter. When it fell to the South Carolina troops on April 12, all hope for nonviolence died as men rushed to sign up "to defend the cause."

Wade Hampton III raised and equipped Hampton's Legion at his own expense, including cavalry, artillery, and infantry. Maxcy Gregg formed the First South Carolina Volunteers. His regiment included 27 physicians and 30 lawyers. They began service at Sullivan's Island in February 1861. There were a total of five companies formed in the town. When Hampton, Gregg, and other companies left Columbia, bands played, banners flew, and hundreds of people lined the streets waving flags and cheering. Talk of victory and a short war dominated conversation with the prevalent opinion being that the north could not exist without the south. Hampton and his men first fought with Jackson at the first Battle of Bull Run. In June 1862, they fought at the Battle of Fair Oaks.

There was a rush of emotion as those left behind did everything they could to support "the cause." Louise T. Wigfall sacrificed her silk wedding dress to make flags for Confederate regiments. The many patriotic gestures of women grew with the war. They nursed the sick, comforted families of the dead, made bandages, knitted socks, met the trains to feed soldiers, helped with homefront industries, and did without niceties.

Abolitionist ideas and conversation were not allowed in Columbia at the beginning of the war. The circulation of the *New York Tribune* was stopped. Julian Selby related that a man named Powell was employed as a stone mason at the new State House site: "He voiced his opinions regardless of warnings and was seized, carried to the neighborhood of Fisher's Pond, his clothing removed and cared for, and he was well smeared with tar, then a pillow case was opened, and he was feathered. He was given his clothing and he left town."

Throughout the war, Columbia was a place of refuge. Banks moved great amounts of money and valuables to the city for safekeeping. Low-country families sent their pre-teen and teenaged sons and daughters to the city to continue their education and to get them out of harm's way. Hotels were filled and relatives sought shelter, causing many private homes to be packed to capacity. As the war continued, refugees eventually doubled the population.

Many schools gained success during the war years and a number of private schools stayed open and conducted an amazing number of classes despite the great difficulties. Many wartime students were from outside of Columbia. Henry Taylor Williams, the 12-year-old grandson of Colonel Thomas Taylor, was sent from Charleston to attend Augustus Sachelleben's school. Upon turning 15 in 1864, Henry was called into service as a sergeant for the last six months of the war.

When the conflict began, the Methodist Women's College on Plain Street was only 18 months old. Reverend Henry Mood had only recently moved to Columbia to serve the college. The school's success came when many families sent their daughters to Columbia. The numbers swelled to 100 day students and 200 boarding students.

The Male Academy and the Female Academy remained as the prime institutions for the early education of the sons and daughters of prestigious families. Richard Ford was in charge of the Male Academy throughout the war. After the war, Hugh S. Thompson directed the curriculum toward classical and college preparatory studies. In 1867, the school was moved to a site donated by Governor John Taylor, which comprised a city block bounded by Richland, Henderson, Laurel, and Pickens Streets. The school was also casually referred to as "Thompson's School." Thompson was well respected and was later elected as state superintendent of education and then governor.

Washington Muller left Columbia, and the Female Academy was put in the charge of Jane and Sophie Reynolds. The war presented lean years, yet to compensate for the uncertainty of the times classes were opened to boys and girls. As the value of Confederate currency fell, tuition was reduced to $4 per month. While citizens attempted to adjust to new living conditions, construction of the new State House continued until 1863. When the war effort required all the state's resources, Niernsee left the state and did not return until after the war.

In October 1861, Gustavus Augustus Follin arrived in Columbia to serve the Confederacy as assistant adjutant general in the South Carolina Adjutant and Inspector General's Office. At the time, States Rights Gist served as the inspector general. The letter from his father dated October 23, 1861 is in the private collection of Mr. and Mrs. Talbot Bissell. It is obvious that his father was not concerned for his safety in Columbia:

Gustavus Augustus Follin (left) served as assistant adjutant general under General Gist. Henry Taylor Williams (right), Colonel Thomas Taylor's grandson, was sent to Columbia at age 12 to attend boarding school. At 16 he joined the Confederate army and served for the last six months of the war. (Courtesy the private collection of Mr. and Mrs. Talbot Bissell.)

Charleston
October 23, 1861
My dear Son,
I am in receipt of yours of yesterday, and am pleased that you arrived safely and in good health, and also that you were so kindly received by friends. Endeavour always my dear Son to cultivate the acquaintance and friendship of all those to whom to be connected with will reflect credit to yourself, and let your deportment be such as to preserve those connections.

You know my solicitations about you and the matters I have endeavoured to impress you with; bear these in mind and act up to them—be careful not to expose yourself in weather, horse riding, etc.—and do not omit attending church.

We all miss you much—but trust our privation is for your good. All send their love to you. We are all well.
Your Father,
G. Follin

By December 1861, there were advertisements offering rewards for deserters. *The Daily Southern Guardian* on December 13 offered a short and simple advertisement: "$30.00

*Wade Hampton III rose to the rank of general. He was a devoutly patriotic Confederate and personally financed the Hampton Legion. (*Harpers Monthly, *February 1865.)*

Reward: Deserted from Camp Huger at Suffolk, VA." The *Regulations for the Army of the Confederate States* covered desertions in Article XIII:

> 99 . . . A reward of thirty dollars will be paid for the apprehension and delivery of a deserter to an officer of the army at the most convenient post or recruiting station. . . . The reward of thirty dollars will include the remuneration for all expenses incurred for apprehending, securing, and delivering to a deserter.
> 101 . . . Deserters shall make good the time lost by desertion.
> 103 . . . Rewards and expenses paid for apprehending a deserter will be set against his pay, when adjudged by a court-martial, or when he is restored to duty without trial on such condition.

Columbia was a boring place for a young soldier to be stationed. Augustus Follin's friend John fought with the Army of Northern Virginia. He wrote to "Gussy" and urged him to come to Virginia and join the action. Follin's mother wrote her son on Christmas Day 1861 begging him not to go. This letter is in the Bissell Private Collection:

> Charleston, December 25, 1861
>
> My dear Gussy,
> I have sent you the gown by Reed. I hope you will be pleased with it. I got the pattern from Mr. Welch. My dear boy, you wrote to your pa about joining the army. Do for heaven sake and ours give up the idea, nothing would grieve

me more and your father too. You are aware that your father will not refuse to advance you when you are in need therefore remain where you are. I think the situation you hold is one of advantage to you hereafter if not at present, if you care for us you must not think of a change my dear boy.

We had a very dull Christmas but notwithstanding that, the boys are firing crackers with a crowd of boys as usual. I wish you a Merry Christmas and a happy New Year. May God bless you and guide you in the right path, those are my constant prayers. Ma and all send kisses to you in haste.

Your affectionate,
Mother

Columbians received news from the front and letters from soldiers on a regular basis due to the town's proximity to the railroad. When there was no news, residents speculated there might be another battle or that the enemy had taken a train. The town also served as a crossroads for transporting supplies and many types of war endeavors were operated. As various industries fell in other areas of the south, Columbia picked up the slack and became a supply base. The entire city put forth a concentrated effort to support the Confederate soldiers.

J.F. Williams was an eyewitness to the wartime activities. In *Old and New Columbia*, he mentioned numerous wartime businesses. A button factory on Main Street made buttons of copper and silver plate. A headquarters for uniforms on Taylor Street cut the fabric and women sewed the garments at home. C.P. Ramsen ran a hat factory that made wool hats for the government. According to Williams, "A.D. Cumpsty said he shaped 250 a day."

The Palmetto Iron Works at Laurel and Lincoln Streets produced cannons and bullets. The State Arsenal was located across the street. The Confederate Powder Mill was established on the Congaree River. A sword factory was located at Main and Elmwood. The Shield's foundry was on Arsenal Hill between Assembly and Lincoln. Shoes for the Confederate soldiers were made on Assembly near Blanding. A uniform factory was located on Taylor Street. Gunpowder was made on the fairground property.

John Alexander ran an advertisement in the December 13, 1861 issue of the *Daily Southern Guardian*:

Congaree Iron Works
John Alexander, Proprietor—Manufacturer
Steam Engines of all sizes
Portable grist mills of all sizes

The Saluda Factory on the Saluda River north of Columbia was one of the last of the large cloth manufacturing operations to remain in business. In December 1855, the facility was purchased by James and Robert W. Gibbes and renamed Columbia Cotton Mill. The Gibbes replaced slave workers with poor whites. By the end of the war, most of the workers were women. Women were also employed to make army socks at the John Judge Company's factory on the corner of Main and Calhoun Streets.

Cloth became a luxury as the south's mills were overly extended making fabric for the troops. Hundreds of old hand looms were put back into service. Ladies bought warp and cotton yarn in 5 pound packages. They'd spin and weave and then bring the finished cloth into Columbia to sell. Many country-women also brought hand-knit socks in for stores to sell.

Four facilities were established for printing Confederate currency, including Keating and Ball on South Main Street and one over Stanley's China Hall. Evans and Coggswell of Charleston set up on North Main Street; Blanton Duncan ran a shop in the Athenaeum Hall. The printing operation set up in an old warehouse on the corner of Gervais and Huger Streets became one of the largest printing facilities in the south. Millions of dollars were printed there.

As the war raged elsewhere, there was a shortage of able-bodied men to work. Women took up the slack and worked in the plant printing stamps and bills. Malvina Gist of Columbia signed thousands of pieces of Confederate money with her own signature, "M. Gist." The $100 note featured the engraved image of Lucy Holcombe Pickens, the wife of the South Carolina governor. Pickens's maiden name of Holcombe was selected for a South Carolina unit: the Holcombe Legion.

For most of the war, Columbia was spared direct conflict. However, trains bearing sick and wounded men arrived daily. The ladies of Columbia established a hospital at the railroad station. It began as a room at the Charlotte Depot on East Blanding Street. It was to be a place where soldiers could rest, have their wounds cared for, and receive meals. The Young Ladies' Hospital Association was begun by Isabella Martin, Sallie Hampton, and Susan Hampton. They were joined by Catherine Macfee and many other prominent high born ladies who volunteered countless hours of service.

The ladies began the first Wayside Hospital in the world. The concept was soon adapted by organized church groups throughout the south. General James Chestnut's wife Mary described her experience at the hospital in her diary:

> Today we gave wounded men, as they stopped for an hour at the station, their breakfast. Those who are able to come to the table do so. The badly wounded remain in wards prepared for them, where their wounds are dressed by nurses and surgeons, and we take bread and butter, beef, ham, and hot coffee to them.
>
> One man had hair as long as a woman's, the result of a vow, he said. He had pledged himself not to cut his hair until peace was declared and our Southern country free. . . . This poor creature had had one arm taken off at the socket. When I remarked that he was utterly disabled and ought not to remain in the army, he answered quietly, "I am of the First Texas. If old Hood can go with one foot, I can go with one arm, eh?"
>
> They were awfully smashed-up, objects of misery, wounded, maimed, diseased. I was really upset, and came home ill. . . . That fearful hospital haunts me all day long, and is worse at night. So much suffering, such loathsome wounds, such distortion, with stumps of limbs not half cured, exhibited to all.

These hospitals served all soldiers and were a godsend to the south for there were few considerations given to regular soldiers when ill or wounded. *The Regulations for the*

The two-story, block long Confederate printing facility still stands on the corner of Huger and Gervais Streets. With the fall of Richmond, much of the currency printing fell to this plant. (Photo by Burke Salsi.)

Army of the Confederate States covered the subject as follows: "The expenses of a soldier placed temporarily in a private hospital, on the advice of the senior Surgeon of the post or detachment, sanctioned by the commanding officer, will be paid by the Subsistence Department, not to exceed seventy-five cents a day." An act to establish Wayside Hospitals at all train stations was passed by the Confederate Congress in 1862. The hospital in Columbia took care of 75,000 soldiers during the war.

The January 18, 1862 issue of the *Daily South Carolinian* gave evidence that the sick and wounded were becoming a serious issue. Dr. R.W. Gibbes served as the South Carolina Surgeon General. He reported the following:

> Under the authority of the Legislature, the Surgeon General has arranged a HOSPITAL for the sick and wounded, in Columbia. It is now open, in a large brick building in the upper part of Main Street.
>
> As there are many articles of necessity and comfort which cannot be bought, any contributions from the citizens of the State will be welcome. The Hospital is open to all in the State, who need medical or surgical assistance.

This hospital was located in the fairgrounds building on Boundary Street. The patients were soon moved to the buildings at the South Carolina College. Julian Mood, Reverend Henry Mood's son, recorded in the family genealogy that a section of the Methodist Women's College was also used for a hospital toward the end of the war. Catherine Macfee was instrumental in having a plot laid out in the Elmwood Cemetery for Confederate soldiers. After Maxcy Gregg was killed in the Battle at Fredericksburg, Virginia, he was interred in Elmwood.

A salt petre plant was established on Dr. Parker's land near the state asylum. All of the refuse of the area was collected and salt petre was extracted. Dr. Joseph LeConte was in charge of the operation and helped to also set up potash works. When the college closed in 1862, LeConte felt the need to use his scientific knowledge for helpful purposes. He established a large medicine factory in the fairground building that had been vacated by the hospital. It included a large scale manufacture of alcohol, nitrate of silver, chloroform, sulfuric ether, nitric ether, and podophyllin. It was a great enough quantity to supply the entire army. In 1864, LeConte was appointed the head chemist for the Niter and Mining Bureau to test nitrous earth in the college laboratory from caves in Georgia, Alabama, Tennessee, South Carolina, Georgia, and Alabama.

By 1863, only the wealthy families ate well. By then citizens realized that their Confederate money was worthless. Assistant Adjutant General Gustavus Augustus Follin wrote to his mother on January 7, 1863: "My own impression is that unless Congress does something to restore the currency to its original value, everything will reach a figure beyond reason and beyond ordinary means."

The poor and average people were lucky to wear homespun and had gone without sugar, tea, or coffee for years. The ladies of the gentry class recycled all of their old gowns. Before the end of the war, few could escape wearing muslin, especially for mourning dresses. Women's hats woven from palmetto leaves became a common sight. Most of the cloth that was available was homespun checks or plaids. Colors were dyed by using pine tops, alder leaves, walnut leaves, and hulls from red sumac berries. A cotton card factory was set up near the State House. Because of the demand, there were many women spinning and weaving. Fine fabric was only available when the blockade-runners were successful. Toward the end of the war, an elegant silk dress cost as much as a carriage. As long as captains risked running the blockades, the rich citizens continued to enjoy bountiful meals and enjoyed attending parties and dances. By contrast in 1863, Mary Chestnut recorded in her diary that a pair of gloves was $30; slippers were $50; six spools of thread were $24; and five little pocket handkerchiefs cost $32. She stated that a basket full of Confederate money would not buy anything.

News that Charleston was under siege created a great deal of interest in Columbia as men and equipment were sent to the front. Gustavus Follin wrote his father the news:

>State of South Carolina
>Adjutant and Inspector Generals Office
>Columbia, July 10, 1863

>My dear Father,
>I have received your letter. . . . As I telegraphed you this morning the enemy commenced an attack on Charleston early this morning. They opened fire from batteries erected on Folly Island the existence of which we knew nothing, I am sorry to say. The Governor received a dispatch this morning stating that after hard fighting the enemy succeeded in effecting a landing on Morris Island. This is very

bad indeed. They must be driven from there or Fort Sumter will be lost to us for there will be nothing to prevent them advancing by parallels and taking position in the rear, just batter away and brick and mortar cannot stand the superior ordnance out and troops have been called for from Georgia and N. Carolina.

We are very busy inventing means of supplying General Beauregard with troops and expect we will have to order out companies badly organized. I would write you more at length but positively have not the time. We expect to be up most of the night. The Governor went down to Charleston tonight.

Write me immediately when you will leave for Charleston. All the negroes in Charleston have been impressed for work on Morris Island.

Excuse this disjointed letter as I write in great haste.

Your affectionate son,

Gustavus

In July 1864, Colonel James Chestnut, a native of Camden, accepted a coastal command after serving as President Davis's adjutant. In July of 1864, he moved his wife Mary into a house in Columbia. In October 1864, Jefferson Davis visited Colonel James Chestnut at his home. Davis arrived with no pomp. Many influential citizens wondered how and why he would skip the honors. Article XXIII in the *Confederate Army Regulations* stated that the

Catherine Macfee campaigned to have a special section set aside for Confederate soldiers at Elmwood Cemetary. A monument was erected to the fallen along with the individual markers for the soldiers who died between 1861 and 1865. (Photo by Burke Salsi.)

President was to receive all standards and colors dropping, officers and troops saluting, drums beating and trumpets sounding. His escorts were to be composed of cavalry or infantry, or both, according to circumstances. They were to serve as guards of honor for the purpose of receiving and escorting the President.

No one, including General Chestnut and his wife, could imagine why the President would not insist on full honors. Mary Chestnut recorded in her diary:

> The President will be with us here in Columbia next Tuesday, so Colonel McLean brings us word. I have begun at once to prepare to receive him in my small house. His apartments have been decorated as well as Confederate stringency would permit.
>
> (The Presidential party arrived before daylight.) Immediately after breakfast, General Chestnut drove off with the President's aides, and Mr. Davis sat out on our piazza. There was nobody with him but myself. Some little boys strolling by called out, "Come here and look; there is a man on Mrs. Chestnut's porch who looks just like Jeff Davis on postage-stamps." People began to gather at once on the street.
>
> . . . The President was watching me prepare a mint julep for Custis Lee when Colonel McLean came to inform us that a great crowd had gathered and that they were coming to ask the President to speak to them at one o'clock. The crowd overflowed the house, the President's hand was nearly shaken off. I prepared for him, with only a Confederate commissariat. But the patriotic public had come to the rescue. I had been gathering what I could of eatables . . . and I found that nearly everybody in Columbia was sending me whatever they had . . . for the President's dinner. Mrs. Preston sent a boned turkey stuffed with truffles, stuffed tomatoes, and stuffed peppers.
>
> Then the President's party had to go. . . . Custis Lee and I spent much time gossiping on the back porch. . . . He spoke candidly, telling me many a hard truth for the Confederacy, and about the bad time which was at hand.

As times got harder, the Methodist authorities notified Reverend Henry Mood that it was his duty to get the boarding students under his charge safely back to their homes. He personally delivered many of the girls as he traveled by horse and carriage, driving as far as Holly Spring, Mississippi.

Camp Sorghum was a reminder that the war was ever present. It was a loathsome place on the west bank of the river that was established as a prison for Union officers. It was named for the main diet: sorghum and bread. In December of 1864, until Sherman arrived, the prisoners were moved to a better, more humane location at the South Carolina Mental Hospital. This decision put the war squarely in the center of the city.

On January 17, 1865, while Sherman was advancing away from Savannah but toward the capital city, Columbians were attending a bazaar held in the Hall of Representatives in the old state house building as "A Tribute to Our Sick and Wounded Soldiers." Citizens donated vast amounts of jewelry and valuable personal items to be auctioned or to be sold. A lot of money was raised through the sale of these items during the festivities.

Dr. LeConte's daughter Emma and her friends worked diligently for weeks planning the event. Emma noted in her diary:

> To go in there one would scarce believe it was war times. The tables are loaded with fancy articles—brought through the blockade, or manufactured by the ladies. Everything to eat can be had if one can pay the price—cakes, jellies, creams, candies—every kind of sweets abound. A small cake is two dollars—a spoonful of Charlotte Russe five dollars. Some beautiful imported wax dolls, not more than twelve inches high raffled for five hundred dollars.

The bazaar was scheduled for two weeks; however, it closed after a few days. By the time word reached the citizens that Sherman was headed toward the city, thousands of people had already arrived from other parts of the state seeking refuge and the city's population more than doubled. They had no idea that while Sherman was in Savannah he had written, "The whole army is crazy to be turned loose in Carolina." He further wrote, "I look upon Columbia as quite as bad as Charleston, and I doubt if we shall spare the public buildings."

His hatred had been expressed many times publicly, through official correspondence and personal letters. It was not a secret that the 61,000 men and officers sweeping through the south with Sherman bore a deep-seated animosity. Sherman's aide-de-camp, Brevet Major George Ward Nichols wrote in his diary that was published in 1865 as *The Great March*, "General Beauregard could not defend Columbia. There were not enough troops and Sherman's troops moved so quickly there was no time to get them there."

Camp Sorghum on the west side of the river was the original site of the Union officers' prison. It was so named for the constant diet of sorghum. The prisoners were moved to the mental hospital in Columbia. (Harper's Weekly, *April 1, 1865.*)

After the fall of Fort Sumter and Charleston, the railroads were so damaged that news of Sherman's advance was not reliable. By January 28, 1865, General Wade Hampton and his men arrived in the city, after serving with General Robert E. Lee and the army of Northern Virginia. On February 15, General P.G.T. Beauregard arrived to organize a resistance. Butler's cavalry of 5,000 was expected to join the force.

Sherman's men poured across the Savannah River after destroying the city of Savannah and only took two weeks to assemble in South Carolina. When General Sherman's troops reached Lexington on February 16, his plan to invade Columbia became obvious. He proceeded toward the river and established a camp at the Columbia Cotton Mill on the old Guignard Plantation.

Citizens panicked as they filled carriages and wagons with furniture and personal possessions. Governor Magrath and other politicians left on the last train out of town. Eyewitnesses stranded in town reported that lines of vehicles could be seen stretched north for miles. Hundreds of bales of cotton were pulled from warehouses and piled in the streets from the railroad depot to the Congaree River. There was a great deal more than usual; the Union blockade of Charleston put a severe cramp in the ability of merchants to get the cotton to European markets. General Hampton was concerned about the bales and placed Confederate soldiers to put out any fires that might start after a direct hit.

On February 14, Emma LeConte recorded that the whole town was in a panic because Yankees were reported a few miles off on the other side of the river. Citizens felt they were safe from attack because of Butler's Cavalry. Yet they were fully aware that Sherman intended to burn the town. By the 15th, Emma recorded that the streets in town were lined with panic-stricken crowds, trying to escape:

> All is confusion and turmoil. The Government is rapidly moving off stores—all day the trains have been running, whistles blowing and wagons rattling through the streets. . . . Hospital flags have been erected at different gates of the campus—we hope the fact of our living within the walls may be some protection to us. . . . It is cold and we have no wood. The country people will not venture into town lest their horses be impressed. So we sit shivering and trying to coax a handful of wet pine to burn. . . . Night! Nearer and nearer, clearer and more distinctly the sound of the cannon. . . . The alarm bell is ringing and I thought at once. It is the Yankees! Of course, I knew it was a fire. I try to be hopeful, but if it is true, as it is said, that this is one of Sherman's army corps, what resistance can a handful of troops make? Oh, if Cheatham's corps would come! Beauregard said he was expecting it in 13 hours, and that was about 2 p.m. They should be here early tomorrow morning.

On the night of February 16, Union troops bombarded the unfinished capitol building from across the river. The cannon balls were unable to penetrate the structure's exterior walls. When the soldiers burned the old State House to the ground, the new granite structure remained intact. Materials relating to the design and construction of the building were lost in the fire or purposely destroyed by soldiers. Julius Mood recorded events of the night:

> It was rumored that the Yankees were coming. On Wednesday, some smoke could be seen in the southwest, and at night the sky reddened like the reflection

*After destroying public property and the railroads for 20 miles, General Sherman crossed the Broad River and entered Columbia. Most of the citizens had fled, leaving mostly women and children to face the Union troops. (*Harpers Weekly, *April 1, 1865.)*

of forest fires at a distance. Occasionally, during the day, sounds of faint thunder could be heard. On Thursday morning, the noise of cannons was unmistakable and by evening we heard that they were across the river. All who could do so were leaving the city in haste. On Friday, the bombardment began in earnest and continued for two days. Shells were dropping into the city every three or four minutes, the casualties, however, were but few.

As General Sherman and General Logan proceeded to the west shore of the river near Granby, Confederate soldiers burned the bridge across the Congaree River as well as the bridge across the Saluda River. Logan's reaction on seeing the bridges gone was that it didn't matter. He would have been wary of crossing the bridge in case it was mined. He traveled with a number of pontoons just for the occasion of river crossings.

As General Sherman's troops approached Columbia, the cadets from the Arsenal Academy were placed in charge of a battery near the Congaree River Bridge. They returned to their barracks and on the night of February 16, 1865, they marched out of town with General Beauregard's troops. The corps marched to North Carolina, then to Greenville, South Carolina, and then on to Newberry, South Carolina. On May 9, the corps disbanded. Sherman's men destroyed the entire campus with the exception of the officers' quarters.

When General Beauregard realized that Union forces were going to enter Columbia, he and General Hampton organized a retreat that began at 9 a.m. on February 17. Hampton requested that Mayor Dr. Thomas J. Goodwyn surrender the city. Confederate officers and city officials hoped that Sherman would spare the city if there was no resistance. The governor, dignitaries, and many well to do people left the city on the last train. When the troops pulled out, the mayor was left in town to "face the music alone," for those who could leave did leave, and in a hurry. Most of the people who remained in town were old people, poor people, black people, women, and children. The able bodied and the wealthy got out of harm's way.

Goodwyn and a small group proceeded toward the Broad River where General John A. Logan laid a pontoon bridge across the Broad River. The mayor formally surrendered to General Stone at Fifth Street and River Drive and assurances were given for the safety and protection of citizens and property. General Sherman crossed the pontoon bridge accompanied by General Howard. The Union troops marched down Richardson Street (Main) to the State House. General Sherman made his headquarters at Colonel Blanding Duncan's new home at 1615 Gervais Street, while General Logan lodged at the Hampton-Preston house. The citizens were somewhat relieved when they learned that Sherman had assured the mayor, "that he and all the citizens may sleep securely and quietly tonight as if under Confederate rule." He also promised that private property would be respected, although he planned to destroy some public buildings.

Emma LeConte heard the news concerning Sherman's arrival from a house servant who rushed in to relate that as the soldiers marched down Main Street, women and children panicked and seemed crazy. Emma ran upstairs in time to see the United States flag run up over the State House. She recorded, "Oh, what a horrid sight. What a degradation! After four long bitter years of bloodshed and hatred, now to float there at last! That hateful symbol of despotism! I do not think I could possibly describe my feelings. I know I could not look at it."

Upon being dismissed, the soldiers began looting and destroying anything they could. Once the Union troops discovered liquor, they engaged in terrorizing the citizens in addition to theft. Drunk soldiers and "hangers on" were empowered by alcohol and

*Union soldiers burned the old State House and damaged marble and granite slabs stacked on the grounds, but they were unable to bring the structure down. (*Harper's Weekly, *April 1, 1865.)*

roamed the streets jerking jewelry from women, demanding watches from the men, and pillaging at will. Nothing was sacred. The troops burned churches, threatened ministers, and were sure to steal the Eucharist silver. At the convent school, St. Mary's College, Father Lawrence O'Connell of St. Peter's Catholic Church reported the college "was robbed, pillaged, and given to flames." It housed 100 students. Jeering soldiers taunted the nuns and blew cigar smoke in their faces. Several men were heard to say: "Now, what do you think of God? Ain't Sherman greater?"

The Union soldiers probed fresh graves for loot. Women who begged for mercy were often beaten and raped. Young children were threatened in front of their mothers' eyes. Residents who failed to reveal the whereabouts of valuables were hanged until they were dead. Emma LeConte noted:

> The Yankees plunder the Negroes as well as the whites. Mrs. Wilson with a babe one week old was moved from her father's burning house. The Burroughs escaped with only the clothing they wore. . . . Some tried to save a little food— even this was torn from their hands. Soldiers taunted helpless women to humble their pride. They'd say, "Where now, is all your pride? See what we have brought you to."

The Mother Superior of the Ursuline Convent and St. Mary's College pled for the safety of the students and the buildings without success. All of the buildings including the rectory with all of the parish records and an extensive library were burned. Reverend Mood's daughter, Mary Catherine, witnessed soldiers cutting up the garden hose. The sisters and the students spent the cold February night huddling behind tombstones in the graveyard while praying for their lives.

When residents begged for help, most officers and guards refused to assist. The destruction began before the troops made landfall in the city. They burned businesses, structures, and destroyed equipment. After arriving in town, soldiers carried out the destruction of the arsenal and the Glaze Foundry. They couldn't destroy the granite State House that was under construction; however, they torched the old wooden state house and it burned quickly. Construction materials that had been left on the ground were smashed. The statute of George Washington located at the foot of the State House was brick batted and the base of the cane was broken off. It was later returned by descendents of the vandals and is on display in the Confederate Relic Room.

Once complete destruction of the city became obvious, both Confederate and Union patients at the college hospital were placed in the middle of the campus exposed to the cold night air. Twenty men died from a combination of fright and exposure.

All of the city's property deeds were destroyed when the City Hall was burned. However, the wills were saved by being hidden in a barn. The City Hall's clock tower was a landmark. It was also the location of the city market, for the building was constructed with open arcades on its first level. Julian Selby recorded in his *Memorabilia,* "as the clock struck one (a.m.), the steeple fell and stopped the echoes summarily."

The Palmetto Ironworks, the Arsenal, and the Powder Mill were among the first properties to be burned by Sherman's men. He wanted all weapons destroyed so that

The "Stars and Stripes" were raised over the battered South Carolina State House on February 17, 1865 after a four year absence. Emma LeConte wrote in her diary that she could not bear the sight. (Harpers Weekly, *April 1, 1865.)*

his retreating troops would not be accosted. The water works was destroyed. The gas works burned when Union soldiers made an attempt to excavate buried shells near the river. The shells exploded and a number of Union soldiers were killed. The First Baptist Church was singled out for burning. The quick thinking sexton, Holland Mitchell, saved it by telling troops that the Washington Street Methodist Church around the corner was the Baptist Church.

Federal soldiers burned the Methodist Church to the ground. It was not rebuilt until 1872. Reverend W.G. Conner was an eyewitness to the crime. He testified that the church was torched three times. Twice he extinguished the flames. During his attempts to save the sanctuary the parsonage was set on fire. He rushed to rescue his sick child. As he ran out with the child wrapped in blankets, a soldier grabbed the blanket and threw it into the third fire that was set. When Reverend Conner made an effort to put out the third attempt to torch the church, the Union soldier threatened to throw the child into the fire.

Trinity Episcopal Church was saved because the name was removed and numerous paper mache crosses were mounted on the parapets. When Union soldiers passed, they felt that only a Catholic Church would have so many crosses. They spared the church because General Sherman's mother was Catholic.

The Lutheran church was torched during Sherman's occupation and the communion silver was stolen. G.T. Berg, treasurer of the church, wrote, "The enemy has left us in a helpless condition. Our provision stores were ransacked and are very limited. We had preaching today in the Sunday School room where a mourning congregation assembled, now deprived of their temple. There were only four copies of the Presbyterian Psalmodist available for the choir." When a new church was dedicated in 1870, the members discontinued borrowing the communion silver from the First Presbyterian Church.

The South Carolina State Hospital's high wall saved it from burning. It was fortunate that it was spared because as the Federal troops departed, over 5,000 homeless people gathered on the property. Dr. R.W. Gibbes's grandson, John Peyre, Jr., was among the group taking refuge at the hospital. He was in the Gibbes house when it was torched and witnessed it burning to the ground. People also took shelter in the buildings on the University of South Carolina campus.

As General J.A. Logan made plans to depart, the Catholic nuns from the Ursuline Convent insisted on using the home as a shelter for members of the order and for their students. Father Lawrence O'Connell personally related the story to Mary Chestnut. She entered his remarks into her diary on March 5, 1865:

> The nuns and the girls marched to the old Hampton house, and so saved it. They walked between files of soldiers. Men were rolling tar barrels and lighting torches to fling on the house when the nuns came. Columbia is but dust and ashes, burned to the ground. Men, women, and children have been left there homeless, houseless, and without one particle of food—reduced to picking up corn that was left by Sherman's horses on picket grounds and parching it to stay their hunger.

Even though the nuns found housing, a few nuns died from complications of exposure aggravated by malnutrition and were buried in St. Peter's churchyard.

During the conflagration, Professor Orchard saved the building of the Methodist Women's College. Despite the unfortunate circumstances, the senior class was graduated in April of 1865. However, the war proved to be the financial breaking point, and the Ursuline Sisters moved into the college building and returned the old Hampton house to the Preston family.

Hundreds of civilians, both black and white, departed with Sherman. They were sent under guard to Wilmington where they sought transportation to northern cities. Marie Boozer and her mother were among them. Columbians had suspected them as Union sympathizers, for they were often seen at the Union officer's prison. Colonel James Gibbes later claimed that he had run into Miss Boozer and Mrs. Feaster in New York where they were pursuing a claim against the Federal government seeking war damages for her Columbia property by attesting to her loyalty to the Union during the war.

The noted author, politician, and respected newspaperman William Gilmore Sims was the editor of the *South Carolinian* newspaper and an eyewitness to the burning of Columbia. He reported that 468 structures including 265 homes were destroyed by Sherman's troops. All of the stores, livery stables, warehouses, and factories were burned to the ground, as well as six churches and four schools. In his book, *The Sack and Destruction of Columbia,* he further noted:

> The best and most beautiful portion of Columbia lay in ruins. Never was ruin more complete; and the sun rose with a wan countenance peering dimly through the dense vapors which seemed wholly to overspread the firmament. Very miserable was the spectacle. On every side ruins, and smoking masses of blackened wall, and towers of grim, ghastly chimneys, and between, in desolate groups, reclining on mattress, or bed, or earth, were wretched women and children, gazing vacantly on the site of a once blessed abode of home and innocence.
>
> Roving detachments of the soldiers passed around and among them. There were those who looked and lingered nigh, with taunt, and sarcasm. Others there were, in whom humanity did not seem wholly extinguished; and others again, to their credit, be it said, who were truly sorrowful and sympathizing, who had labored for the safety of family and property, and who openly deplored the dreadful crime, which threatened the lives and honors of the one, and destroyed so completely the other.

The citizens who survived Sherman's occupation were desperate for food and shelter. Julian Selby shared a humorous note in his *Memorabilia:*

> Soon after Sherman's departure, we found ourselves in the fix of the boy, who is described as diligently digging for a length of time in search of a ground hog. When the suggestion was made that he couldn't find the animal, the indignant reply was, "I've got to have him; the preacher is coming and there's no meat in the house."
>
> We were out of that necessary provision, when a solitary pig came in sight. Chase was made, but the animal had passed through that experience before; he turned and ran in different directions, but finally we over hauled him in what I supposed was the neighborhood of his home. About the time he gave his last squeal, a colored woman came up and claimed the carcass. As we had chased the animal fully an hour and had several falls, as he back-tracked and ran between the legs of some of the parties in pursuit, bringing them to the ground, his claimant agreed that we should make an equal division. Adding, "Dat pig was de debbil. Soldiers run him, weuns run him and youuns run him; tank God, he dead, sure!" We dined on fresh pig that day.

Emma LeConte wrote, "Standing in the centre of town as far as the eye can reach nothing is to be seen but heaps of rubbish, tall dreary chimneys and shattered brick walls. . . . The wind moans among the bleak chimneys and whistles through the gaping windows of some hotel or warehouse."

The Mood family had no food and no prospects of staying in Columbia. A friend in Union County sent a wagon and a team to transport the family to Goshen Hill. Reverend Henry Mood loaded the wagon with as much as possible and sent his wife, daughter Mary

When it was all over, Sherman left no buildings standing in the main part of the city. Union troops smashed much of the granite and marble stored on the State House grounds. This photo looks north up Main Street.

Catherine, and other children to stay with the friends. Mood and his son Julian then set off by foot. They walked the 60 miles with a sack of field peas and a milk cow. Julian recorded that while they were attempting to ford the Congaree River on a raft, the cow jumped off and swam back to the Columbia shore. After three attempts, they managed to get her to the proper shore and were able to resume their long walk.

When Columbia burned, the war was over for the citizens of the town. All of their energies were consumed with survival. The Chestnuts left Chester, South Carolina and headed to Columbia on May 2, 1865. Mary noted her impression of the landscape in her diary entry: "Since we left Chester nothing but solitude, nothing but tall blackened chimneys, to show that any man has ever trod this road before. This is Sherman's track. It is hard not to curse him. I wept incessantly at first."

5. RECONSTRUCTION

The Civil War gave slaves their freedom, yet it left them adrift without a vision or leadership to help them establish a future. They knew they were free and could go anywhere they wanted to go. However, most had nowhere to turn. Even if they had a place in society, most were without skills to support themselves. Reconstruction gave them a time to establish themselves in various endeavors since only the free blacks had developed marketable skills before the war.

The confusion that gripped the city following the war worked against early efforts to survive. There was no food and shelter. Looters carried off all of the valuables and money they could get their hands on. Those left with Confederate currency found it worthless. Governor Magrath moved the legislature to Greenville. With the city decimated by Sherman's troops, there was nowhere to go but up—for everyone.

Mayor Goodwyn appealed to Sherman to leave 500 head of cattle so that the citizens would not starve. He did leave cattle—the ones that had not fed for days and were walked to death. Many cows died before they could be butchered; others did not have meat on their bones. All 7,000 people in town were starving. Some families were helped by loyal servants and slaves who found ways to secure food. The lack of communication to the outside world presented a temporary problem. Friends and family in other towns sent aid. Some burned out families left town to live with relatives. Reverend Henry Mood sent his wife and young children in a wagon to Union. Since their milk cow had been spared, Mood and his son Julius walked the 60 miles leading the cow and carrying a bag of peas.

Only one gristmill was left in town. Doctor Joseph LeConte used a flat-boat on the river that had belonged to the Niter and Mining Bureau to haul corn from plantations. By March 7, other towns fully understood the state of things in Columbia, and wagon loads of goods poured in.

Goodwyn soon resigned his office. The *Phoenix* reported on May 27, 1865, that J.G. Gibbes was given the position of mayor by the council. Gibbes appealed to other towns for aid. There were problems in receiving the help that was offered, as communication lines had been cut and the railroad had been completely destroyed, often with tracks twisted around trees and beyond repair. Help came by wagons from Augusta, Charlotte, Chester, Greenville, and Sumter, as well as many other small communities throughout the state. Food was provided for 7,000 people a day for three months. When loads of supplies were stolen before they could be delivered, citizens appealed to the governor for help.

It was difficult for officers of a lost war to return home. Their lives were shattered, their homes destroyed, and their fields decimated. Some felt that there was no way to support themselves or their families. Many once wealthy young men from the planter class returned to find themselves penniless and socially displaced. Once well off, citizens were homeless and experienced the same crushing poverty as the poorer classes. Some felt they were about to get on their feet politically speaking, when the hand of the military governor and the Republican Party took over. They were deposed along with all conservatives and members of the old guard.

The *South Carolinian* changed its name to the *Columbia Phoenix* and was the only newspaper to rise from the ashes of the city. William Gilmore Simms was the editor, Julian Selby served as the publisher, and Dr. R.W. Gibbes, Sr. was the owner. It was difficult to find the paper, press, ink, and other tools necessary to produce an issue. Somehow Gibbes obtained the items and on March 21, 1865, the first edition was printed. It carried the front page headline, "Sack and Destruction of Columbia." The paper continued almost the entire period of Reconstruction. After Dr. Gibbes died at the age of 57 and Selby began a printing business in 1876, the paper was discontinued.

Construction began at once—homes, businesses, transportation lines, the gas plant, churches, government offices, and schools were rebuilt. Eighty-eight blocks were destroyed and ruins were everywhere. It was essential to provide shelter for hundreds of displaced people who lived in rigged shelters, outbuildings, public buildings, or by sleeping on the floor of the few homes that were spared. Blackened chimneys and fragile, scorched brick walls framed new construction. Washington Street Methodist Church built a chapel by salvaging bricks from the burned sanctuary. In his book, *Tried By Fire,* Archie Vernon Huff, Jr. pointed out that there was no money to purchase lime for cement, so the bricks were held together by red clay mortar. The few places spared included Trinity Episcopal Church, First Baptist Church, the Hampton Preston homes, the Marshall DeBruhl house, a few houses on Arsenal Hill, the unfinished State House, the mental hospital, and the college buildings.

Wade Hampton was the richest man in the state before the war. Following the surrender, he returned to find his plantation ruined, his home burned to the ground, and debts of

*The buildings on the grounds of the State Mental Hospital were not burned and provided shelter for thousands of Columbians after Sherman left the city. Union officers held as prisoners were freed from the site. (*Harpers Weekly, *April 1, 1865.)*

more than $1 million. All of his personal belongings were sold at auction, and through the help of friends he bought a small house in Columbia.

On May 29,1865, President Andrew Johnson issued a proclamation of amnesty to those who pledged loyalty to the U.S. Constitution. He introduced his Presidential Plan for Reconstruction and South Carolinians hoped that things would quickly return to normal.

In the spring of 1865, representatives of the newly formed Freedmen's Bureau attempted to come to the assistance of the poor persecuted and untrained former slaves, but there were too few agents, too little cooperation, and too few jobs. By May, conditions improved; cotton supplies found a market, and northern merchants once again offered credit to old southern clients. Some citizens left and traveled abroad and others discussed emigrating to Mexico or Brazil. Wade Hampton refused invitations of asylum in foreign countries, even when the Venezuelan government offered him a 2,500-acre land grant. William Gilmore Simms wrote in the September 14, 1865 issue of the *Columbia Phoenix,* "We have succumbed, we are submissive. There is not a dog among us so conceited as to suppose he has a tail at all."

The South Carolina College obtained a new charter in December 1865 and became the University of South Carolina. Schools of law and medicine were added, using the University of Virginia as a model. Former professors, including Joseph LeConte and his brother John, returned and students came from disbanded army units. During the Reconstruction years, the university was forced to integrate, but did not allow female students. A normal school was opened on the campus and trained black females to become schoolteachers. Dr. LeConte was only paid a $2,000 per year salary. In his autobiography, he labeled the situation "intolerable," especially when he discovered that the 5 percent tax of $100 placed on his income was more than the entire legislature paid in taxes. In August

General Wade Hampton returned from the Civil War to find his plantation in ruins and his home burned to the ground. He and his family lived in this small house known as Southern Cross on Taylor Street. The general is pictured standing in the center.

of 1869, Joseph LeConte became a professor at the newly formed University of California and moved from the state.

A series of events occurred that brought the city to its knees. The Congress of the United States refused to seat the representatives from southern states. It did not help when the south was reluctant to adopt the Fourteenth Amendment of the Constitution granting slaves civil rights. The U.S. Congress voted down the President's Reconstruction plan and adopted the Reconstruction Acts of 1867 that enforced harsh controls over the old Confederacy. Each state was forced to draft a new state constitution and hold new elections for public offices. Occupation forces arrived to oversee all facets of life in the south; states were stripped of all authority.

The state and its citizens were put under federal military rule in July 1867 and became part of the second military district. The military was headed by General R.S. Canby, who served as the commander. He was responsible for protecting life and property, as well as for the relationship between planters and freedmen. Troops patrolled the town and curfews were imposed. The military took over the university, forced out professors, and squandered funds. "Carpetbaggers" took over and hired professors that were described as adventurers. Treasury agents were like vultures as they questioned citizens and acknowledged all accusations. For 11 years, the U.S. government did not consider the residents of Columbia to be citizens of their own country.

Obtaining food and shelter and making a living proved to be difficult for all classes of people. Landowners did not view the military as helpful, especially when the army tried to incite freedmen to riot. In other cases, the army would favor punishing lazy workers. By 1867, sharecropping became the system used by the planters and the freedmen. It provided incentives by giving a share of the crop to the workers; sharecropping helped the landowners because it did not require cash transactions. However, it was unfortunate that the crops of 1866, 1867, and 1868 were substandard. The summer drought of 1866 was disastrous for the cotton crop and added to the strain of farmers, workers, and the banks. The formerly wealthy as well as the poor workers nearly starved. These struggles caused new patterns of agricultural management to emerge. Laborers ultimately became unwilling to remain subservient.

In 1867, the Union Army supervised elections for representatives to the new state constitution convention. White politicians of the old guard attempted to stop the meeting and the drafting of a new document. Thomas Gibbes and L.D. Childs traveled to Washington, D.C. and appealed to the Reconstruction Committee but were ignored. The convention met in Charleston on January 14, 1868 with 76 blacks and 44 whites serving as delegates. Only four were Democrats; 116 were Republicans. Forty-four members of the delegation came from the north. It changed the districts into counties with each county to have one senator, except Charleston, which kept two. Representation in the House of Representatives was based on population and stipulated that office holders did not have to be property owners. It further stated that public education was to be provided for all races. For the first time, women were given control of their own property and divorce became legal. The final document turned out to be amazingly fair and democratic.

The Democrats held a convention in the First Baptist Church to elect a candidate for governor. Hampton was drafted, but declined the nomination realizing that there was the possibility of retaliation because of his service to the Confederacy. He was listed on the ballot; however, the "carpetbagger" candidate, James L. Orr, a former member of the U.S. House of Representatives, was declared the winner. Among his early duties in 1867 was assigning Reverend William Martin of the Washington Street Methodist Church to survey the extent of suffering among the population. Martin submitted a report revealing that 1,670 people were being fed by charity.

The northern Republicans organized Union Leagues to influence African-American voters and control the elections. In many ways, though, South Carolina became more democratic. Prior to the war, only the white wealthy male property owners could vote. The poorer classes and blacks had no influence or vote. To the dismay of the old political class, Reconstruction stripped away their power and influence. For the most part, they sat on the sidelines and witnessed the new government officials mishandle funds and rig elections.

The African Americans who made great strides assumed positions of responsibility in all levels of government. Many were empowered to improve their lives and to influence the lives and hopes of others. From 1867 to 1876, over one-half of the office holders were black. Others were from out of town and included carpetbaggers and scalawags. General Canby ordered that African Americans be seated on juries. A Columbia barber, Christopher Haynesworth, was the first to serve. Also included was Jonathon J. Wright, a free black man who graduated from the University of Pennsylvania. He became a South Carolina state Supreme Court justice. Francis Cardozo graduated from the University of Glasgow in Scotland and was appointed the state treasurer and secretary. Robert Smalls, a former slave, served in the state legislature and five terms in Congress. Although S.B. Thompson was a barber, he also gained political prominence.

Many Federal Reconstruction authorities were little more than hoodlums on the public payroll. Some who became influential with the military government used state funds to finance favors that led to personal gain through a system of pay-offs. Columbia had a white majority and the county had a black majority. After the mayoral election in 1868, General Canby removed the elected mayor, J.T. Zealy, and all of the aldermen. He replaced those elected with people he favored. After this, the legislature extended the city limits so that African Americans would be in the majority in the city.

The first Republican Party in Columbia was founded in 1867. Members of the Freedman's Bureau, free blacks, carpetbaggers, and scalawags organized it. These efforts encouraged African Americans to become involved in politics, and blacks helped form Republican clubs throughout the state. Although most of their actions were unfavorable, they endorsed many good things including public schools and helping landless farmers. Several necessary social and public works projects were successfully completed.

From 1867 to 1874, the county court was held on the second floor of Carolina Hall. The ground floor was the general store of James G. Gibbes. Finally in 1874, a new courthouse and a new town hall were erected with public funds. The town hall had offices and an opera house but no market; McKay's store was located on the first floor. It was thought to be inferior to the one burned by Sherman and citizens disliked the architecture. When citizens learned of the actual cost of the construction, they knew that all of the money was not spent on the court building. The need for a bridge across the Congaree River was urgent. Nothing had been done since the bridge was burned in front of Sherman's advance. In December

*President Andrew Johnson served as the military governor for Tennessee. South Carolinians hoped his proposals for Reconstruction would be adopted, but they were not and the entire south suffered under military law during the Reconstruction years. (*Harpers Weekly, *April 5, 1865.)*

1872, a new bridge 5 feet higher than the old one was opened over the Congaree. It operated as a toll bridge, yet it was much more convenient than the ferries.

There was a great deal of concern surrounding the completion of the State House. The building's architect, John Niernsee, returned to Baltimore during the war to resume his practice with his former partner, James Crawford Neilson. The Reconstruction legislature met at the South Carolina College through 1867 when a temporary roof and interior partitions were finished in the State House. Gas pipes and lighting were also installed and the interior was completed enough to make occupancy possible.

In 1872, one of the most notorious Reconstruction governors, Frank J. Moses, Jr., and his wife paid $15,000 down and moved into the Hampton-Preston mansion. Moses gained the reputation as the "the robber governor" because he mismanaged public funds and kept much of it for himself. J.F. Williams was a Columbia resident at the time and remembered Moses as "the worst scoundrel." He related in *Old and New Columbia* that on at least one occasion Moses was a prisoner in his own home: "A warrant was issued for his arrest, yet he had his home guarded by a company of Negro militia to prevent the arrest." Eventually, Moses served time in prison for theft.

Moses was but one of the northern politicians who sacked the state. The federally run council applied to the legislature for authority to issue $25,000 in bonds under the guise of rebuilding the city. The indebtedness was increased to $850,000 over four years. Only $75,000 was accounted for. Many methods were employed to divert public funds into the hands of schemers and carpetbaggers, even though many public works and buildings needed attention. By 1870, the Congaree Bridge had not been rebuilt and flat boats were used to facilitate crossing. The only people who benefited from the misplaced goals of the scalawags were the shop owners, prostitutes, and the 40 saloon owners.

In 1868, Reconstruction Governor James L. Orr declared the old officer's quarters at the abandoned Arsenal Academy to be an excellent location for the home of the governor. The building had served as a boarding house off and on and was virtually uninhabitable; however, the site high on Arsenal Hill provided an excellent view of the city and also of the river. The General Assembly provided appropriations to transform it into a residence and Governor Robert K. Scott was the first governor to move in during 1869. Through the years, many improvements have been made. Electric lights were installed in 1894 and Governor John Gary Evans was living in the house in 1897 when porcelain toilets and bathtubs were installed.

The post war demand for wood attracted northern lumber barons. The reconstructed railroads were expanded and were used to move produce and commercial goods, thereby stimulating new markets. Transportation and new technology also increased the demand for cross ties, trestles, telegraph poles, and lumber for houses and for furniture. Steam powered sawmills increased production to 150,000 board feet per day. By 1909, more lumber was cut in South Carolina than in any other state. The railroad also attracted timber business by opening inaccessible areas. Makeshift narrow gauge railroads called tramlines were built and extended to the point of logging. As trees were felled, the railroads moved the logs to the sawmills and then moved the sawn lumber to market.

A line to Augusta bypassing Branchville was planned before the war, but construction did not begin until 1867. No progress was made in standardizing rail construction; therefore, trucks had to be changed before cars could be transferred from one track to another. There was no standardization until 1886.

Establishment of the South Carolina State Penitentiary on the east bank of the Columbia Canal in 1867 was the most progressive social project begun during Federal occupation. Because of the inhumanity of old laws and the abysmal conditions in local jails, the legislature debated the establishment of a prison system for over 70 years. By the Civil War, the state recognized 165 offenses that were punishable by death. A prison system meant that offenders might have a chance to be rehabilitated. The first two cell-blocks and an administration building were constructed of local granite by prison labor. In 1901, the first building was remodeled and a tuberculosis hospital was built. Throughout the decades, various industries were created to give inmates work skills. Between 1870 and 1900, many handcrafted items were sold in town to add to the revenue of the facility. Inmates in the early 1900s worked at prison owned farms and the institution operated at a profit.

Missionary groups worked for the education of African Americans, and education for all citizens gained importance. In 1870, the American Baptist Home Mission Society, through the philanthrophy of Mrs. Bathsheba Benedict of Rhode Island, established Benedict Institute. Benedict purchased 8 acres of a plantation east of Columbia to establish a college to train newly emancipated African Americans as teachers and ministers. The first pupil was a 66-year-old minister; nine boarders and thirty day students followed him. The first school building was a large two-story home on the site that was once owned by a slave-owner. The building was referred to as the "mansion."

The African Methodist Episcopal Church moved the Payne Institute from Cokesbury to Columbia in 1880 and established facilities near Benedict College. The school was renamed Allen University in honor of Bishop Richard Allen, the founder of the African Methodist Episcopal Church, the first church in America exclusively for African Americans. The establishment of Allen marked the first time that blacks had a facility of higher learning. In the beginning, Allen prepared students from first grade through college. The college graduates were prepared for careers as school teachers and preachers. Arnett Hall was constructed in 1891 and originally housed all of the classrooms and offices. The Chappell Building of 1922 was designed by John Anderson Langford, who was known as the dean of black architects. The building was named for W.D. Chappelle, a president of the university.

A provision for education was written into the Constitution of 1868 and the office of state superintendent of education was created. Reconstruction brought a great deal of confusion to the educational system of Columbia. Most of the established schools managed to stay open even though they were forced to lower their tuition. Classes were also held in private homes and were mostly taught by women. This proved to give the youth a decent basic education and met the economic needs of the teacher and of the students. Various new private academies were begun. Sisters Isabella and Margaret Martin opened the Columbia

Inmates at the penitentiary were put to work. Some worked constructing the penitentiary and the State House. Others farmed and fed the entire prison population. The South Carolina Penitentiary Boot and Shoe Factory opened to provide useful products to the population. Photo c. 1880.

Columbia College was moved into the buildings above in 1905 from downtown after 40 acres were donated for a campus. The campus was reconstructed after a 1909 fire. This 1905 postcard view shows the original campus.

High School for girls. At the time, there were only two public schools operating prior to 1881. Programs for white children were under the control of the Sidney Park School; the Howard School sponsored classes for black children.

In 1866, Washington Muller returned to Columbia and opened the Columbia Female Seminary and competed for students with his old school, the Columbia Female Academy. Despite the desperate times, he stayed open until 1873 and eventually taught the children of many of his former pupils. Mary Ann Buie, who collected money for "wounded soldiers" during the war, moved her school from Edgefield in 1870. Her "hook" to attract students was by advertising that she was "the soldier's friend." She accepted her paying students and provided a few scholarships for Confederate orphans. When she did not meet with success in Columbia, she moved to Aiken in 1872.

After the Ursuline Sisters moved from the Methodist Women's College, T.S. Nickerson operated Nickerson's Hotel in the property through 1872. The college trustees then raised enough money to reopen the school in 1873 in the same building. The institution grew and in 1894 added programs in advanced math and science so that the school could compete with other schools of higher learning. When the college outgrew its facilities, F.H. Hyatt and Colonel J.T. Sloan donated 40 acres for a new campus a few miles north of Columbia. The new campus was open in 1905, but was destroyed by fire in 1909. The students moved back to the old building in town and boarded for a year while the campus was reconstructed.

While a few colleges were closed during federal occupation, the theological seminary continued. Thomas Woodrow Wilson moved to the city in 1870 when his father joined the college faculty. The family moved to a house on Pickens Street while a new home was built on Hampton. The boy known as "Tommy" became the 28th U.S. President.

The Columbia residents never did "catch-on" to federal occupation and as the years passed, the resentment grew. For years, evidence of Sherman's conflagration remained in the form of lone scorched chimneys. On one of General O.O. Howard's visits to Columbia, he met General Wade Hampton accidentally in the presence of Major James G. Gibbes. Julian Selby described the incident:

> The Major introduced the two generals. Howard promptly put forward his one hand towards the Carolina General, who withheld his for a few seconds, saying, "I cannot take your hand, sir, until you retract your statement as to my connection with the burning of this city."
>
> "General Hampton," was the prompt reply, "I freely admit that I was mistaken in that matter; and hope that now you will forgive and forget it." Hampton nodded and a hearty handshake resulted.

As the election of 1876 approached, many conservatives discussed supporting the incumbent, Governor D.H. Chamberlain, a Maine "carpetbagger" who had made some attempts at reforms. Just as the Democrats were coming to terms with Chamberlain as a candidate, the legislature appointed the former governor, F.J. Moses, Jr., to serve as a judge on the circuit court. Those "sitting on the fence" joined the Democratic faction that was determined to rid the state of the military government.

The Democratic convention met in Columbia on August 15, 1876 at the old State Fair Grounds. Wade Hampton was nominated as a candidate for governor. Although he had lost his wealth, Hampton was held in high regard, because of his service to his city and state. During the gubernatorial campaign, citizens paid him the respect and admiration due a war hero. His friendly relations with African Americans and his sincerity gave him rapport with all audiences. Hampton's followers organized a movement of political soldiers to boost his presence throughout the state. N.G. and Ambrose Gonzales, Colonel A.C. Haskell, and Colonel James Chestnut were among the first men to join the Red Shirts.

Their campaign cry was "waving the bloody red shirt." This was a reminder of those who fought and died during the War Between the States. Colonel Haskell handled the campaign while Hampton "stumped" all over the state. Crowds of Democrats waving red shirts attended the meetings. They demanded equal time and took every opportunity to discredit the Republicans. They took pains to avoid violence and made the campaign boisterous, including yelling down opponents. However, they avoided rousing the ire of the U.S. commander. The up-country farmers became hostile to Governor Chamberlain and out of fear he avoided certain sections of the state.

Demonstrations were staged in Columbia and a mile-long torchlight parade wound down Main Street. Two hundred and ninety former rifle clubs reorganized in support. The Columbia Flying Artillery was among the rifle clubs that supported Hampton even though they were ordered to disband. They resurrected themselves as the Hampton and Tilden Musical Club. The clubs clashed with the militia at political meetings and caused several near riots. Throughout the election process, and especially on Election Day, fraud was rampant. Blacks threatened blacks, whites threatened whites, whites and blacks threatened each other, and a partisan line was drawn between the Republicans and the Democrats.

On Election Day, November 9, Hampton won by a small margin. Chamberlain refused to concede and accused Hampton of corruption. Both the Republicans and the Democrats claimed victory. On December 7, 1876, Daniel H. Chamberlain was inaugurated governor. That same night, Hampton made a speech and said, "The people have elected me governor, and, by the Eternal God, I will be governor or we shall have a military governor."

When the legislature assembled in January 1877, troops were stationed at the State House. Hampton and the other fairly elected Democratic representatives were refused admission to the building. Representation in the Senate was composed of a Republican majority; they, therefore, claimed an official victory. The Republicans reorganized the House without the Democrats and elected a speaker. The Democrats withdrew to Carolina Hall, located near City Hall, and formed a totally Democratic House of Representatives. William Wallace was elected as speaker. They finally slipped into the State House. For four days, both the Democratic House and the Republican House met side by side. When the Republicans became violent, the Democrats left.

Because Florida, Louisiana, and South Carolina agreed to cast their electoral votes for presidential candidate Governor Rutherford B. Hayes during the election of 1876, the Compromise of 1877 took effect when Hayes took office in March. Wade Hampton III was named the officially elected governor of South Carolina. Hayes put a Southerner in his cabinet. He immediately withdrew troops from the south and urged congress to appropriate funds for the construction of a transcontinental railroad that would use a southern route from New Orleans to Los Angeles.

When Reconstruction was over, Columbians felt the radicals had been dethroned. Hampton became the symbol of a new era. With his assent to the governor's office, many of his supporters were appointed to powerful offices and worked to restore antebellum ideals. Hampton brought renewed interest in the state and imbued confidence in local businessmen. New life came to the city when improvements were made, new businesses opened, and social events revitalized. New ideas were unleashed as every effort went into building for the future.

After being elected governor, Wade Hampton was not allowed to take office and serve in the State House. Instead, the Democrats met in Carolina Hall before Hampton was recognized as the legitimate governor by the President.

6. A NEED FOR CHANGE

The spirit of the Civil War was kept alive well past the turn of the twentieth century in honor of the thousands of brave men and women who served and fought for the "lost cause." Hampton's election signaled the end of the Republican hold on government and the end of diversification in politics. There was a renewal of the old romanticized notion of military heroism reminiscent of the prewar and war years. The Richland Volunteer Rifle Company resumed their drills and parades, one of the political and social outlets until the late 1890s.

When the call came to fight the Spanish in 1898, four training camps were organized to receive soldiers from all parts of the United States. Camp Ellerbe was set up at Hyatt Park, Camp Dewey at Geiger's Spring, Camp Fitzhugh Lee in Shandon, and Camp Prospect at the fairgrounds. Camp Fornance was established as a brigade headquarters when the government recommended that troops in cold climates be relocated to Columbia. Soldiers were sent from Pennsylvania and marked the first time in the city's history that hundreds of non-southerners descended upon the city. The young men added a lively dimension to the social scene and also added to the local economy. Special events occurred weekly, including parades, parties, concerts, dances, and church socials. The success of the project so impressed local businessmen that businessmen led by Edwin Robertson appealed to Washington for the establishment of a division headquarters. The request was not accepted, but Columbia leaders did not forget the importance of having the military in town.

The years between 1880 and 1900 were focused on the struggle of the population to get beyond muddy streets, weed filled vacant lots, a struggling economy, and strangled educational institutions to become part of the new south. Governor Hampton closed the University of South Carolina from 1877 until 1880 in order to regain control of the school and revitalize its faculty and curriculum. It reopened for whites only and was renamed the South Carolina College of Agriculture and Mechanics. It was not re-integrated until 1963. In 1882, the name was changed back to the South Carolina College and it became the University of South Carolina in 1887. In his annual message to the General Assembly in November of 1890, Governor J.P. Richardson praised the university, its faculty, and students for their "vitality and efficiency." Richardson unknowingly affected the status of the school when he called for the legislature to set aside appropriations to assist in the establishment of an agricultural college.

Ellen Elmore served on the cusp of a new era of education when she took over the Columbia Female Academy in 1879. For in December of 1880, the General Assembly

During the Spanish-American War, Columbia became the location of several military camps and Camp Fornance. The view above shows soldiers marching north on Main Street. It must have been a dry day because the water wagon can be seen halfway up the street headed in the opposite direction.

declared the City of Columbia to be a separate school district. They provided for a board of school commissioners consisting of one member from each of the city's four wards and a fifth member to be selected by the city council from their own members. There were only two public schools in the city at the time. By 1883, both the male and female academy transferred their land to the City Public Schools.

Between 1881 and 1883, the public school session was only three months long and the majority of the students were African-American children. When a special tax to support the school system came up for a vote in 1881 and again in 1882, citizens voted it down. At that time, the only funds available for schools including buildings, upkeep, equipment, and teachers was $1,700. With Colonel F.W. McMaster as the chairman of the school board, the commissioners set about organizing a system. The biggest hurdle was getting the ordinary citizens of the community interested in the idea of education for all children. The well to do families looked at the schools as a place for paupers, and the poor citizens felt too proud to accept charity. Many felt that an education was wasted on children who needed to work full time and help support their family.

The question of a tax to support schools was raised again in 1883. The public wanted to be assured that tax money would in fact be spent on developing good free schools. Charleston was used as an example. At the time, eight percent of their children were enrolled and only four percent were in school in Columbia. It was also proposed that the school term be extended to nine months. Colonel McMaster again sincerely appealed to the population to support a school tax. He finally roused them to vote "yes." After this, McMaster was thought of as the "Father of Columbia Schools."

Columbia was at least 30 years behind compared with cities in northern states. The economy had barely improved when the panic of the early 1890s affected the state, carrying many problems and concerns over into the new century. Bankruptcies occurred when the price of cotton dropped to only 4¢ per pound. A new group of tenant farmers was created when two-thirds of the state's small farmers lost their land because they couldn't pay their taxes and their debts. Every facet of life suffered.

Construction of the State House lagged for almost 35 years and the structure was not complete. Only two modern conveniences were available: telephone and gas lighting. Newly installed but ugly telephone and telegraph poles marred the appearance of the streets. Ainsley Hall experimented with making gas at his office on the corner of Lauren and Main Streets as early as 1821 and was the first to install gas lights in his residence on Blanding Street. The Columbia Gas Light Company was chartered to make and sell gas for the needs of the city. The effort lasted until 1865 when Sherman burned the plant. When rebuilt in 1871, a serious effort was made to construct lines throughout the city. By 1888, gas lights illuminated all of the churches, most of the hotels, the State House, and some homes. Street lamps were installed on Main and Sumter Streets. Before dark each evening, a lighter rode his horse to each lamp, stood in his saddle, and lit the flame.

The coming of the telephone was not much less complicated. A telephone exchange opened in 1880. It was a disappointment when only 27 subscribers signed up for service out of a population of 13,000. The exchange was located on the second floor of the Central National Bank Building (later known as the Sylvan Building) on the corner of Hampton and Main Streets. By 1881, there were 60 members on line between 10 a.m. and 6 p.m. Twenty-four hour service was made available except on Sunday in 1883. In 1910, the crank telephone became obsolete and individual users communicated with the operator by saying, "Hello central." Columbia became the second city in the United States to be completely on the dial system in 1922.

Citizens had serious misgivings about the efficiency of the archaic water works and the safety of the water. It was pumped by a steam engine from an underground spring to a steel holding tank known as the "standpipe." It then flowed to homes by gravity through iron pipes. The steel tank was the only major improvement since Blanding constructed a brick holding tank in 1832. An act of the legislature in 1890 made money available to improve the water works through new construction and equipment. The new operation included water pumps and filters to clarify the muddy water and to remove pollutants.

The project was a failure because of the lack of knowledge of filtration. Straight polluted and muddy water continued to be pumped into homes. People bought bottled water for drinking or they boiled city water. In the summer of 1897, Dr. William Royal Stokes, a bacteriologist, was brought to Columbia to analyze the water supply. He pronounced the water to be exceptionally good. In spite of the report, citizens remained concerned about the water. They were also aware that there was no proper sewer system. The city had a large population, eight hotels, fourteen churches, three banks, boarding houses, and retail businesses. There was no hospital and the public health was thought to be in danger.

In 1883, Niernsee returned to Columbia to prepare a report on the work needed to complete the State House. He resumed his position in 1885, but he died six months later. James Crawford Neilson took over his partner's work and followed the original designs.

He was replaced in 1888 because of his refusal to move to Columbia. Frank Niernsee, John's son, took over. He is noted for completing the interior of the building and for salvaging much of the original Tennessee marble that his father had ordered in the 1850s for the "great marble hall." He added several details of his own to the main lobby, stairs, and gallery. He completed his father's work in 1899.

Frank Pierce Milburn, another noted architect, stepped in from 1900 to 1902 and completed the porticos, rebuilt the roof, and added the exterior and interior domes. The building was wired for electricity and new fixtures were added. The legislature was so dissatisfied with the quality of Milburn's work that they sued him and had Charles Coker Wilson take over the job of correcting Milburn's mistakes in 1903. He spent two years between 1905 and 1907 reinforcing the roof and then covering it with slate. He improved the exterior doors and began the process of landscaping the grounds.

Within a few years of Reconstruction, the citizens of Columbia resumed the pursuit of pleasure. They renewed their interest in travel, theatre, balls, and dances. They ventured forth to the coast, to Charleston, and to the mountains. Those who traveled to New York had bragging rights. Those who took a European trip had a lifetime of conversation and a certain status among their friends. Yet most citizens were delighted with the return to normalcy. Citizens could sit on their piazzas, enjoy the breeze, work in their gardens, visit neighbors, and hear the gentle tinkle of cowbells coming from the pastures on the edge of town.

The State Fair was resurrected at the old fair grounds on Elmwood Avenue in 1869. At the end of Reconstruction, "fair week" returned with daytime events and entertainment for all ages, including harness racing at an adjacent racetrack. At night, the fun moved downtown where the streets were illuminated with gas lamps. Crowds walked up and down Main Street and visited carnival tents at Lady, Washington, Hampton, and Taylor Streets. There were band concerts, special performances at the theater, and the Elks Club sponsored an annual parade.

Everyone eagerly awaited the fair. To many people it was bigger than Christmas, and plans for parties were made from year to year. It was socially acceptable for the week to accentuate ease. It was a vacation of sorts in a time when vacations were only for the rich. Hotels published their guest lists in the daily paper so that residents could get in touch with out of town friends and relatives. The streetcar company was overworked and added additional tracks to accommodate the crowds. In October 1905, *The State* published a defense of the fare increase from a nickel to a dime because the construction of additional tracks made the fare hike necessary.

The September 7, 1900 issue of *The State* covered the fair and reported that people had arrived from all over the state. The reporter added, "confetti tossers will be everywhere and young and old will go in for a real good time." The State Agricultural and Mechanical Society of South Carolina incorporated as an eleemosynary institution and moved the fair to a space south of the city on Bluff Road in 1904. In 1908, the fair society purchased a metal building from Greensboro, North Carolina that had originally been used at the Jamestown Exposition. The building was renamed "the steel building" and was used for Columbia's state fair week for over 50 years.

Football became a fair week attraction. Intercollegiate games began in 1891, when Carolina played Furman College. In 1896, the football teams of the University of South Carolina and

Clemson College began a 63-year tradition of playing each other during the State Fair week. The games were played at Melton Field on the university campus. Residents of Columbia enjoyed the convenience of walking through the State House grounds to arrive at the game. The games were suspended in 1902 after Carolina beat Clemson and a fight erupted between the students. Violent conduct was not acceptable; the competition did not resume until 1909. The Carolina–Clemson game became the biggest sports event in the state and became known as Big Thursday. It was played on the Thursday during fair week. Students were dismissed from school and received free admission to the fair. Stores on Main Street closed and those without tickets were considered unfortunate. The contest ended in 1959, when Clemson felt that it should be played in Columbia only every other year.

Frank P. Milburn designed and constructed the new city hall on the corner of Main and Gervais Streets, directly across from the State House in 1900. The brick façade featured two identical towers flanking the main entrance, except one tower housed a town clock with four faces so that it would be visible from all directions. City offices were located on the first floor and the remainder of the building was used as an opera house also known as the Columbia Theatre. It was the largest social hall in town with 600 seats. It attracted professional acts from throughout the United States. The management regularly presented vaudeville, plays, musicals, operettas, and operas. During fair week, the theatre hosted an entire week of shows, mostly musical comedies.

As the handsome new building was rising on Main Street, a move was underfoot to do away with Sidney Park. The Seaboard Air Line Railroad needed land for a terminal facility. A group of businessmen backed by City Council members overrode citizens' appeals to save

The Elks' Parade was an important event during the annual State Fair. These ladies are riding in a flower-decked horse drawn carriage decorated for the 1902 ride down Main Street.

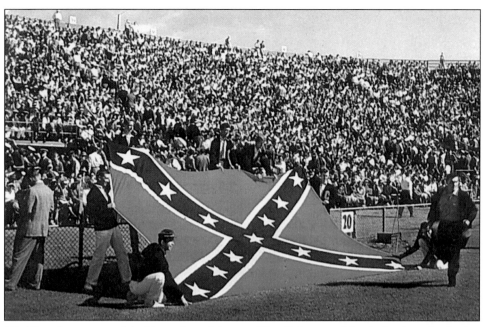

Big Thursday was one of the biggest days of the year. The University of South Carolina cheerleaders traditionally brought out a gigantic Confederate flag at half time. This photo dates c. 1950.

the park. The railroad paid $30,000 for an indefinite lease and destroyed the beautiful public recreational space. Railroad sidings and warehouses replaced flowers, trees, and walkways. In the name of progress, Seaboard Park became an immediate eyesore in the heart of the city.

Edwin Robertson's new mansion on top of Taylor's Hill was under construction. He was perplexed to have the unsightly facility at the bottom of the hill and used legal means to save the park. Unfortunately, the case did not reach court until after the railroad had altered the space. Robertson bought the land adjacent to his new home and donated it to the city. In 1909, he purchased the property along Assembly Street from Laurel to Elmwood and created a parkway that became known as Robertson Parkway. After Assembly Street was paved, this section was closed to traffic and Columbians skated in the street in the 1930s.

Edwin G. Seibels joined Robertson in the quest to beautify the city. A Civic Improvement League was formed to discuss the future look of Columbia. F. Wellington Ruckstuhl, the sculptor of the Wade Hampton Memorial, met with the group in 1904 and suggested not allowing buildings in the town to be erected over 80 feet except for steeples and spires. Since the "skyscraper" had already been erected, Ruckstuhl suggested building another tall building across the street as a symbolic gateway to the State House. He also recommended sand clay streets, stone curbs, street signs, decorative lampposts, and garbage collection.

It was almost ironic that the Chamber of Commerce stressed the need for parks in 1911. This led to 15 acres in McCreery's Bottom becoming Maxey Gregg Park. In 1912, Valley Park was established at the site of the old Shandon Pavilion. Irwin Park was built in 1913 at the water works only to meet with a setback during World War I when the city felt that the thousands of men at Fort Jackson might overtax the water supply and plans were underway to expand the water works. The zoo was dismantled, but the bulk of the project was cancelled when the war ended. After the war in 1919, Earlewood Park was established. Hyatt Park became Victory Park on May 19, 1919, and the first public swimming pool was built. The park purchased 800 bathing suits and a family could swim an entire season for $50.

The need for public inter-city transportation came to a head in 1882, when Columbia's population reached 10,000 and the city area was pushed past the original planned inner city. On February 9, 1882, the Columbia Street Railroad began the use of single or double tracks "of such gauge as they may elect through any street or streets of Columbia." The operation began with 6 cars, 30 horses, and 4 miles of track. The system carried an average of 800 passengers per day. The office, stables, and car barns were located on West Gervais Street.

Electricity replaced the horses in 1893; however, horses were kept on standby in case of an electrical failure. Reliable transportation sped the development of neighborhoods beyond the city limits. The streetcar expanded and Columbia's suburban neighborhoods developed rapidly. Eau Claire, north of Columbia, was the first to develop at the end of the line. When Columbia College moved to the area, the streetcar made a turn in front of the main building. In 1895, a beltline was constructed extending north on Harden Street to Gervais, then west to Main and returning to Valley Park by way of Blanding, Gregg, Taylor, and Heidt Streets. Riding the beltline became a popular family outing on Sunday afternoons. The car company constructed a casino on the edge of the town near present day Five Points. Dances and other events held at the casino encouraged additional riders for these occasions.

During this period, the board of trustees of the original Columbia Male and Female Academies agreed to lease their respective buildings to the Columbia School Board to conduct a nine-month public school term. In return, the academy gained the right to name two members to the board of school commissioners. Ceremonies on September 28, 1883, marked the first day of the term. The boys gathered at the Male Academy and the girls and younger boys gathered at the Female Academy. The black students, both male and female, went to the Howard School. The event was described by a school report reprinted in *The Columbia High School Story, 1915–1975* by Russell Maxey:

> The city bell struck 13 strokes at 8:30 a.m. as a warning, and in obedience to the summons, the children began to flock to the several school buildings from every quarter of the city. Promptly at 9 o'clock, opening exercises were held in every school room. Until 2 o'clock, the regular routine was maintained with the addition of special recitations. Provision had been made in advance for every pupil who entered. 550 whites and 380 blacks presented themselves on the first day and were accommodated without delay, confusion or inconvenience.

The new system was far more successful than the two previous years, and the idea of public schools caught on. However, the system didn't have enough money to improve the buildings, pay teachers, and still allow a free education. Soliciting donations, staging fundraisers, and charging students in grades 8–10 a fee of $2.50 per month almost solved the problem. The younger pupils attended at no charge. Non-resident students in all grades were required to pay. Even with all the efforts, the superintendent could not cover a nine-month term. In April, he set a small fee for students who wished to continue. Lower grades paid $1 a month and grades 8–10 were raised to $5 a month. In December of 1884, the public voted to pay a school tax and students no longer had to fund a public education.

Superintendent Johnson envisioned the creation of a program for upper grades. He suggested that a high school be established in the Female Academy building. In 1895, E.S. Dreher became superintendent of education and the Washington Street School, the first high school, opened with a three-year program of study for both sexes. C.E. Johnson served as principal and teacher and was joined by Fannie C. McCants and P.G. Bonham.

On November 2, 1904, academy properties were conveyed to the public school system in perpetuity as long as the academy members could appoint two members to the school board. It was agreed if the property ceased to be used for a school or for educational purposes, the land and buildings would revert to the Columbia Academy. From that time forward, the Academy ceased to exist, except to name two members to the school board.

The Taylor School was the first modern school building constructed and was considered a milestone in the development of educational facilities. It was built on the site of the Columbia Male Academy on the corner of Pickens and Blanding Streets and was named for the Taylor family who had originally donated the property. It was the first modern school building erected in Columbia. It was followed by the McMaster School in 1911. The Logan School was built in 1913 on Elmwood Avenue on the old fair ground property, and the Blossom Street School opened in 1916. Plans for the Logan School began in 1904 when Charles Logan donated 4 acres and $40,000 to be used to erect a school for white children. The land was to be made available at the death of Mrs. Logan; however, she released the property in 1912 so that the school could be built with matching funds from the school district.

Margaret Autrey attended Taylor School. She recalled that students learned classical poetry, reading, writing, and arithmetic:

> We had our hands and nails inspected for cleanliness everyday by our teacher, Miss "Jack" Wright. My third grade teacher, Miss Talley, was particular to assign the seating according to what each family was capable of contributing to the class. Mary Stork's father owned Stork's Florist and she sat at the front of the class, because she brought fresh flowers to the teacher.

Wardlaw Junior High was the first Junior High in Columbia. It opened in 1926 and was the first school to offer cafeteria lunches. Margaret Autrey said:

> We thought that we were up town. My mother gave me a quarter a day and I could buy five things. Each item including milk, meat, vegetables, and dessert were a nickel each. It was fun deciding how to spend my money. Sometime I would save back a nickel to help finance a trip to the movies on Saturday.

Miss Grace Sease, Miss Seawright, and Mr. Barton were among the first teachers. Barton was known for his two-seater automobile. Yet Margaret Autrey recalled how he gleefully failed students who did not complete their work. By far, Sarah Godbold, the tall, lean, and lanky gym teacher, was the most remarkable and best-remembered teacher at the school.

The State on September 9, 1915 featured the letting of the contract for a new high school and a sketch of the building's design. The headline read, "Handsome New Columbia High School." The article included:

> The school was let at a meeting of the public school board held yesterday afternoon in the office of E.S. Dreher, superintendent, to George W. Waring, a Columbia Contractor. The successful bidder's offer was $97,979.
>
> . . . It will be a handsome structure of three stories designed with a feeling for the Italian renaissance. The arrangement is modern, aiming especially for the health and comfort of the teachers and pupils.
>
> On the ground floor there will be manual training, cooking, sewing, and bookkeeping departments, class rooms, gymnasium, toilets, cloak rooms, and heating plant. . . . The auditorium will seat 850 persons and, like the entrance halls, will have ornamental plaster work.

The cornerstone was laid on November 24, 1915 in a traditional Masonic ceremony. It began with a procession from Craven Hall on Washington Street led by Brother Jesse T. Reese, Grand Marshal, and the Columbia Mills Cornet Band. High school students sang "America," and Governor Richard I. Manning spoke.

Margaret Autrey attended Columbia High School between 1929 and 1932. She recalled many experiences. During her school career from 1921–1932, female teachers had to

The Taylor School was built on the site of the Columbia Male Academy in 1896. It was the first elementary school in the city to offer modern facilities and a nine-month school term. It was named for Governor John Taylor, son of Colonel Thomas Taylor, who donated the square of land for a school.

Margaret Autrey is shown with her aunt Elma Goss Lowrey at Mrs. Lindsey's house on Third Street near Park Street. Margaret and her friend were students at nearby Wardlaw Junior High School.

be unmarried. They were also excluded from positions of leadership and barred from many professions:

> Students in Miss Gertrude Foster's homeroom knew her reputation. She was a strict disciplinarian and didn't put up with anything. She was thought to be as old as Methuselah, but children lucky enough to have her for math, learned their lessons or else. She knew everybody in town, because she had taught them or their parents and not many students dared to cross her for fear she would call their parents.
>
> The Civil War was a lively topic of conversation, but that was because it was still considered a fairly current topic. Miss Clayton, the eleventh grade history teacher, was known for her knowledge on the subject. Her students knew if they said, "Miss Clayton tell us about the war," she would get wound up for the rest of the period. Of course, she blamed the north for the war. She got going on northern aggression and that was only half of it. She knew all of the girls in Columbia who married Yankees. In my day, if you married a northerner, you had transgressed.

Columbia High served as the only high school until 1937, when the suburbs expanded and Dreher High School was constructed on the site of Paul R. Redfern's old airfield.

As the new century dawned, women found it nearly impossible to enter traditional male occupations. They were met with ridicule and resistance. It took perseverance to be allowed to enroll in traditional male dominated colleges. Other than clerical work, teaching was one of the few jobs women were sought to perform. Gradually they became allowed to study nursing and social work. They played a role in the development of libraries and thus became librarians.

By 1895, the city's 30-year post war recovery was miraculous. The streets were lined with trees and state institutions were in place with jobs for hundreds of people. The railroads crisscrossed on Gervais and South Main in every direction. A month after the turn of the twentieth century, the Seaboard Railroad from Cheraw arrived as the ninth railroad service. No other city could compete with Columbia's level of rail service; the city was again on top as a market center. Columbia maintained the same depots on Blanding and Gervais Streets since the first train arrived in the 1830s. When the Seaboard arrived, passenger facilities were non-existent. The Columbia City Council prevailed upon M.L. Bonham, the railroad commissioner, to encourage the four roads leading into the city to join together and erect a proper station that would also promote passenger travel.

The Southern Railroad and the Atlantic Coast Line joined together and opened Union Station on South Main Street on January 14, 1902. The Seaboard Railroad continued service from the old station on Gervais. The railroad was a lifeline for the city through peace and wartime. Hundreds of troop trains arrived and departed as thousands of young men arrived to train at Fort Jackson during two world wars.

Toward the end of the century, several efforts were made to honor fallen heroes. Isabella Martin, an early supporter of the United Daughters of the Confederacy, was instrumental in raising money for a Confederate monument to place on the State House grounds. N.G. Gonzales was helpful in publicizing these efforts in *The State* newspaper.

In December 1895, the Wade Hampton Chapter of the United Daughters of the Confederacy organized the South Carolina Confederate Relic Room and Museum in the State House. They collected artifacts for the purpose of memorializing the service of the South Carolinians who fought in the War Between the States. In 1905, the State of South Carolina agreed to assume the financial support of the museum. Thousands upon thousands of school children of many generations remember taking the requisite field trip to visit the displays during their elementary and junior high years. Margaret Autrey visited in 1922, her daughter Lynn Sims in 1955, and her grandson Jay Swygert in 1979. When the collection outgrew the State House, it was moved to the World War Memorial Building. In 2002, it was moved to the State Museum on Gervais Street, where a modern gallery was constructed. Margaret's grandsons, Bo and Brian Salsi, were the first to sign the guest book on opening day.

When General Sherman published a memoir in 1892, it was read with interest. For years, there was a question in the minds of Columbians considering the origin of the burning of Columbia. Sherman blamed the origin of the inferno on Wade Hampton. Those who knew General Hampton felt that he would have never willingly caused the fire, yet there was nagging doubt. To the relief of the citizens of the city, Sherman wrote, "In my official report of this conflagration, I distinctly charged it to General Wade Hampton, and confess I did so pointedly, to shake the faith of his people in him, for he was in my opinion boastful, and professed to be the special champion of South Carolina." Friends, followers, and believers in the general were relieved. He was vindicated within his lifetime.

In 1905, Julian Selby summed up Reconstruction and its immediate aftermath in his *Memorabilia*:

> By 1905, notwithstanding Sherman's attempt to "wipe us out" we have almost 40,000. Real estate has doubled and tripled in value, vacant places been and being built upon, a skyscraper towers over us, mills and manufacturing of many different kinds are carried on successfully, emigrants come in. We communicate with the world and the rest of mankind by means of telegraph and long distance phone. Railroad connection is complete with every section, besides river communication with the sea. Trolley lines connect suburban settlements and in the near future Brookland, Lexington, and other neighboring towns will have these convenient modes of transportation. Columbia is fast losing one of her principal attractions—the beautiful gardens.

Union Station was constructed south of the State House in 1902 at a cost of $150,000. The facility served as a freight depot and provided a modern, comfortable terminal for passengers.

7. Decades of Progress

The war was blamed for every missed step in the efforts to resurrect a fine antebellum-type lifestyle for the citizens of Columbia. With the turn of a new century, it became more and more difficult to blame the war for everyday realities. Violence remained a holdover from Reconstruction, and murders and lynchings were not unusual. Most young men carried pistols. At times, sections of Columbia seemed like armed camps. Prosecutors had a difficult time convicting murderers because many jurors believed that the victims deserved it.

South Carolina was one of the wealthiest states in the nation in 1860. By 1890, it was nearly the poorest. The situation was exacerbated because there were no public hospitals, no public libraries, a weak public health system, and only two public schools for each race. This set the scene for Benjamin Tillman, a large landowner from the western part of the state, to enter politics. While campaigning for governor, he focused on the misfortunes of the farmers—collapsing farm prices, the oppressive credit system, and the agriculture department. He called it "a sop to Cerberus, a bribe to maintain the support of the farmers in the Legislature."

Tillman championed the discontented. He stirred up old and bitter feelings by debating the 100-year-old class struggles between the up-country and the low-country. He spoke to the ordinary man in a time when all classes turned out to hear orators. He used every colorful phrase possible to emphasize his ideas and aggressively proved his points of view. His forcefulness earned him the moniker "Pitchfork" after he proclaimed that he wanted to "stick a pitchfork" into President Grover Cleveland.

Tillman was fed up with the low-country politicians. He lambasted Charleston leaders and made constant referrals to the "greedy old city of Charleston." He disdained traditional institutions as he sneered at "the broken down aristocrats." He referred to the Citadel as "the dude factory" and to the University of South Carolina as "the seedbed of the aristocracy."

Wade Hampton was viewed as a savior until the day he died; however, his clinging to pre-war ideals worked against him. In his run for re-election to the U.S. Senate in 1890, Tillman portrayed Hampton as "a Bourbon" and the leader of an unprogressive generation. Past glories became irrelevant in the world of the common man who worried about getting food on the table, and Hampton was defeated by John R.M. Irby. His supporters considered the defeat a great indignity.

Farmers appealed to the legislature for aid and their entreaties were ignored. They looked for a spokesman to advocate a government overhaul. Ben Tillman was their man. During his campaign, he played up class prejudices with comments that roused the audiences such as "I am simply a clod-hopper like you are." The "old guard" dismissed him because they underestimated the power in the numbers of voting blacks and poor whites.

Benjamin Tillman attacked the state's political leaders as "do-nothings." He recommended creating an agricultural college to educate the sons of farmers; a Farmer's Association was formed to support the proposal. The idea might have died had Thomas G. Clemson not willed his estate and $80,000 to establish an agricultural college. Clemson College was created in 1891 and took over the agricultural courses offered at the University of South Carolina. The idea appealed to the disenfranchised residents in the upper sections of South Carolina. They felt that Columbia and Charleston had been the bastions of government long enough. All citizens were not happy about a second state-funded college; however, they felt that an agricultural school made sense.

Tillman was passionate about leaving the "old days" behind and his ideas appealed to those who agreed that the state was in a rut. By 1892, the dictatorial governor had commanding majorities in the General Assembly and took control of the state government, ignoring the voters. Tillman's philosophy dominated political thought for a decade. He was elected governor in 1890, re-elected in 1892, and then served as a U.S. senator.

During Tillman's reign, the university returned to college status and struggled to survive. The university board simplified the curriculum, reducing the number of courses offered from twelve degrees to four: classical, literary, scientific, and law. President McBryde moved to Virginia and enrollment declined dramatically. In 1894, there were only 68 students. A plan was formulated in 1895 that allowed women to attend. At first, they were limited to select courses. Professors and male students who resented the co-educational environment created a critical, hostile atmosphere. A few women persisted; in 1898, the first women graduated. In 1905, when the South Carolina College celebrated its centennial, it was again granted a charter as the University of South Carolina, which became official in 1906.

The State newspaper was established in 1891 to thwart Tillman's political efforts, despite the already established *Columbia Register* and the *News and Courier*. Factions against Tillman joined N.G. Gonzales in launching an anti-Tillman newspaper. N.G. and his brothers despised the politics of "Pitchfork" Ben and agreed to establish a paper with the backing of 107 stockholders. N.G. resigned his position as a reporter with the *Charleston News and Courier* and invested $1,000 he had saved for a vacation. He enlisted his brother Ambrose to raise an additional $30,000 by selling advertising and subscriptions.

They purchased a press and set up a plant in a storeroom in the old city hall The press was run in the basement by seasoned newspaperman Julian Selby. Their goals included publishing the largest newspaper in the state and publicly exposing Tillman's schemes.

Ironically, the first issue of *The State* was published on Wednesday, February 18, 1891, four days after the death of General Sherman. The issue contained articles of state and national interest including news of the Johnstown flood. The general's demise was uniquely reported:

> *The State* is glad that it did not have the duty of commenting upon the life
> and character of General Sherman. To have eulogized him would have been

The State *succeeded in putting* The Register *out of the newspaper business by 1892. The Gonzales brothers were competitive and worked tirelessly to create the largest newspaper in Columbia.*

impossible, and to have dealt, while he lay in his coffin, with the lurid chapter of that life associated with this city would have been deemed ungracious. Silence is preferable and History shall speak.

The Gonzaleses upheld many worthwhile campaigns that served their community, the state, and the people. They also upheld honoring veterans and civic heros.

Governor Tillman proved to be more ruthless than the Gonzales brothers had predicted. During the years he held office, *The State* referred to him by 37 unflattering labels, including "baboon" and "buffoon." Tillman referred to the newspaper as "that rattlesnake down on Main Street."

His most notorious act was taking over the State Dispensary. The public supported prohibition, yet when the bill was put before the legislature, Tillman slipped in an alteration that created the dispensary. The dispensary system of selling liquor gave the state government a liquor monopoly. Tillman supported the dispensary as a temperance system and as a revenue source. When the dispensary bill passed, *The State* newspaper reported, "more offices for the obsequious, great profits for a few favorites, inconveniences for the public at large, special privileges for the elect."

105

Women were allowed to attend South Carolina College in 1892. Well-dressed Gibson girls are seen above strolling across the University of South Carolina horseshoe. The Jonathon Maxcy monument in the foreground was designed by Robert Mills in 1827 to honor the first president of South Carolina College.

The liquor monopoly was unpopular in many towns, especially in Columbia. Some felt that it went too far when various patent medicines were removed from the market for having a high alcohol content. Among the 41 products prohibited was Peruna, which was advertised as a cure for catarrh of the head, throat, lungs, stomach, kidneys, bladder, and female organs. *The State* newspaper printed: "Goodbye, Peruna! Fare Thee Well, Hosletter's Stomach Bitters; Henceforth Thy Name is Booze!"

There were rumors that constables were appointed to search homes for liquor without warrants. In Darlington, citizens rioted after the dispensary constables roughed up citizens and fired a shot into a crowd, killing an innocent bystander. This began the Dispensary War. Tillman declared Florence and Darlington Counties to be in a state of insurrection. He called out the militia to control the disturbances and riots. Tillman planned to impose a press censorship and placed soldiers at telegraph offices. Militia members in Charleston, Columbia, Manning, and Sumter refused to report for duty. The governor then called companies from Edgefield and Newberry, posting them at the State House, the Dispensary warehouse, and the governor's mansion. The action lasted only a week, yet the episode fueled a greater division in the political groups throughout the state and particularly in Columbia.

The circulation of *The State* doubled that of the *Columbia Register* in 1894, but still it was not as large as the *News and Courier*. In June 1897, Charles Calvo of the *Register* became ill and his paper was sold at auction. *The State* printed, "Here endeth the first lesson." However, their joy over the demise of a competitive paper was short lived. George R. Kaester, a former editor of the *Register*, began an afternoon paper, the *Columbia Evening*

Record. By 1910, *The State* became the largest newspaper in South Carolina with a circulation of 14,519.

Tillman was open about his desire to weaken the black vote and counted on the conservative Democrats to feel the same way. While the party was courting black voters, Tillman called for a constitutional convention and proposed literacy tests for all voters. The black and white rural delegations vehemently opposed the measure. At the time, African Americans were part of the town's activities. They attended theatre, and their patronage was welcome in shops and stores. Tillman's action was divisive and the precursor of decades of unfair politics, double-dealing, prejudice, and deceit directed toward the black population.

The 1895 constitution set the stage for suppressing fairness. When combined with the new election laws, the force of the black vote and the poor white vote was eliminated. To make matters worse the first of the Jim Crow laws were passed, and for decades the black population became more and more disenfranchised. These actions did more harm than good, for without the black vote so many factions were created that the Democratic Party was skewed and gentrified. There were mill workers that Tillman referred to as the "damned factory class," the growing middle class, the landowning small farmer, the displaced tenant farmers, and the working class. Tillman began the establishment of a society based on color. While he was in power, he made sure that segregation became state law. The city's black population was on the way to gradually becoming disenfranchised.

After his election, Tillman admitted to more rational thinking about the South Carolina College, but only after he reduced the school to the level of a small college. He encouraged legislative support to keep the college open, yet pressed his conviction that there should be different institutions of higher education, not just one "grand university." The ultimate benefit of his support helped to establish other state funded colleges, including Clemson College, Winthrop Normal and Industrial College for women in Rock Hill, the Colored Normal, Industrial, Agricultural and Mechanical College in Orangeburg, and the Citadel in Charleston.

In 1893, Tillman recommended allowing women to attend the South Carolina College. He said that it was "a matter of justice and common sense in keeping with the spirit of the age." At a time when everything seemed to be going downhill, the faculty was directed to admit women to all courses of study in June of 1895. Frances Guignard Gibbes was the first female to enroll. After clashes with the state government, limited curriculum and decreased student body, the move was seen as a temporary measure to increase enrollment. Co-education was not well received by male professors who felt that females might disrupt the progress of the male students. For years, the right of women to receive diplomas was questioned. Few females attended from outside of the city, for there were no dormitory facilities. A room in a private home cost as much as $15 per month and was considered very expensive.

During the last year of Tillman's term, N.G. Gonzales published a series of editorials taking Ben Tillman's nephew, Lieutenant Governor James H. Tillman, to task over the irregularities of the governor's office. The outspokenness of *The State*'s editorial staff helped to defeat "Pitchfork" Ben in his run for governor in 1902. They labeled him the "worst and most indefensible man who ever sought the Democratic nomination."

On January 15, 1903, just before his term was to end, the lieutenant governor crossed Gervais Street from the State House to the northeast corner of Main Street with friends. He encountered N.G. Gonzales, who was walking home for dinner. Tillman pulled out a gun and shot Gonzales in front of his friends and other witnesses. The editor faced his assailant and according to eyewitness published accounts said, "Shoot again, you coward." Gonzales underwent surgery, but died four days later at the age of 44.

Tillman's attorney was successful in getting a change of venue and the murder trial was held in the Lexington County Courthouse in Lexington, west of Columbia. Tillman claimed that Gonzales was walking with his hands in his pocket and he thought he detected a menacing move. Tillman claimed self-defense and was acquitted. Among *The State*'s headlines was "A Testimony of Perjurers."

With the death of Gonzales, *The State*'s fight for many causes, including compulsory education and the abolition of child labor, were put on hold. It was years before effective strides were made in these areas. On December 12, 1905, an obelisk was erected by Gonzales's friends across from the State House grounds and set on the island at the intersection of Senate and Sumter Streets. It is the only monument built to honor an American newspaper editor.

Hampton's death in 1902 was a blow to the entire state and was reported in newspapers throughout the eastern states. With his death, there was no doubt that the "old days" were over and that a "new day" had begun. On the occasion of the Confederate Reunion in Columbia, the *New Bern Journal* of New Bern, North Carolina, ran an article on Sunday, May 17, 1903. The headline read, "Empty Saddle Headed Parade":

> A feature of the parade of the Confederate Reunion in Columbia, S.C. was the appearance at the head of the procession Gen. Wade Hampton's aged body servant leading the beautiful horse the general rode on his last public appearance in the reunion procession two years ago.

In 1906, Hampton was honored when an equestrian monument was dedicated on the State House grounds. Ten thousand people gathered for the ceremony. Hampton's death indeed marked the end of an era.

Civic progress was part of a project of boosterism to better the overall condition of the city. The old buildings of the Methodist Women's College were leased to the developers of Columbia's first resort hotel. Ambrose Hampton was among the group that felt Columbia needed a modern, large facility to serve travelers, politicians, and businessmen. The Colonia Hotel's opening on January 15, 1907 was well publicized.

A new police station and barracks were built behind the new city hall. In 1910, an automobile patrol wagon was purchased to supplement the department's four horses and four bicycles. A new police station and jail were built at 1415 Lincoln Street east of Main Street, next to the county jail. It became known as Kramer's Hotel, a reference to the chief jailer, Marion Kramer. Officers walking a beat called in to headquarters over call boxes located around the city. They reported "all is well" or called for "black Maria," the department's black van, to take lawbreakers to jail.

The streetcar staff is pictured in front of the transfer station at Main and Gervais Streets. N.G. Gonzales was shot near this corner, while walking home from his newspaper office, which was located in the middle of the same block just beyond the Capitol Restaurant sign.

Many new businesses were begun as the population increased, and young men were attracted to the opportunities in the capital city. Educated and skilled men found many avenues open to them as they became involved in law, banking, politics, brokerages, new industry, and helping to establish schools and hospitals. However, the poor white and poor black people had few choices. Most were trapped in menial labor or on rural farms with few chances for success. There were many barriers relating to race, gender, inadequate education, and ethnicity. It is no surprise that approximately 50,000 African Americans left South Carolina to find work in northern and western states during and after Reconstruction.

This loss in population was a blow to Columbia and in 1880, South Carolina attempted to attract immigrants. According to information published by The Jewish Historical Society of South Carolina, Charleston had the largest Jewish population in America by 1800. From there, Jews migrated inland with many settling in Columbia and, through the years, helping to attract new families. The push for immigrant citizens increased the population and the new Jewish residents brought their skills to benefit the community. At first, many came as peddlers, bakers, shoe makers, journalists, clerks, and shopkeepers. They stayed to also become doctors, lawyers, bankers, and businessmen. The names of Levy, Berry, and Lourie continue to be associated with the commerce, leadership, and success of Columbia.

A liberal Jewish congregation formed the Tree of Life Congregation in 1896. It was first known as "a Liberal Orthodox Congregation." Their first building was constructed on Lady Street in 1905 and the Reform program was adopted. The new sanctuary on Heyward Street was used from 1952 until 1986, when a temple was built on Trenholm Road.

In 1907, a synagogue was constructed by the Beth Shalom congregation on Hampton Street. The Columbia Hebrew Benevolent Society established a cemetery close by. In the mid 1930s the congregation built a larger house of worship and the old building gained fame as the Big Apple Night Club. The dance known as "The Big Apple" was invented there and Columbia experienced a small degree of fame as the dance swept the nation.

Columbia attracted immigrants who brought special skills and talents to the area. They formed communities, formed alliances with other new residents, combined southern culture with their individual heritages, helped to establish new faiths, and helped to establish new Columbia traditions. Most of the stone masons who worked on the State House in the 1850s and many who toiled to build the Columbia Canal were Irish Catholics. They established the Catholic faith in the area. Scottish, Swedish, and German families were also well received beginning as early as the 1840s. The Scottish were active and both Dr. Edward Heintsh and P.G. McGregor owned drug stores. An Irishman by the name of McKenna opened a tavern and did well serving the Irish workers. A Bureau of Immigration was created and 294 immigrants arrived by 1894.

The Sylvans were a skilled family of jewelers and watchmakers who emigrated from Sweden in the 1890s. Emil and his brothers changed their name to Sylvan after arriving. Laura Sylvan Sims' father owned a beautiful home on Senate Street. He conducted his clock repairing and watchmaking business from the basement. In 1905, his brothers moved their business into the Central National Bank building that was constructed on the corner of Main and Hampton Streets in 1871. When Margaret Autrey married Frank Sims, Laura Sylvan Sims became her sister-in-law. Dr. T.A.W. Elmgren married another one of the sisters, Hannah, and located his optometrist office in a second floor office in the Sylvan Building that could be accessed on Hampton Street.

As Columbians ended the nineteenth century, they experienced over a decade of uncertainty. As they were immersed in a changing world, there was a struggle. Old feelings did not die easily and the citizenry was denounced by north and south as being stuck in lethargy and laziness. The state in general and Columbia particularly faced various woes of poverty, illiteracy, and lack of motivation. In the late 1890s, South Carolina was one of the poorest states in the country.

Sanitation was among the many problems that had to be addressed. Horses and mules pulling wagons and carts remained the principal conveyances for hauling goods and general transportation. Each horse deposited 20 pounds of manure and half of a gallon of urine on the city streets each day. That meant that 53 tons of manure a day had to be dealt with. It was a must for every business and every home to have a foot scraper by the front door.

Public health became a serious social issue. The unsanitary conditions added to the likelihood that tuberculosis, malaria, whooping cough, and smallpox would infect the population. Women could not vote. Those who had vision and compassion campaigned for temperance, hospitals, education, and libraries. The child labor law of 1903 received their support and the tuberculosis treatment center was a result of the support of the South Carolina Federation of Women's Clubs.

At the turn of the twentieth century, there was no hospital. Although the first State Board of Public Health was created in 1879, it was not until after 1900 that medical professionals, educated citizens, and government joined together to address health issues. Governor

By 1893, the streetcar was electric and Sylvan Brothers had moved into the bank building on the northeast corner of Main and Hampton. Bicycles gained popularity and were quick and reliable transportation.

Coleman Blease did little to promote public health and the progress of medicine. Doctors did what they could to educate the public in sanitary methods. James Wood Babcock, the superintendent of the State Mental Hospital was active in diagnosing pellagra and urged the support of the public health service.

In 1920, the State Board of Health sponsored campaigns to decrease malaria, pellagra, and hookworms. Their theme was based on prevention that required citizens to change their traditional behavior. Other common illnesses included influenza, typhoid, and yellow fever. The influenza epidemic of 1917 resulted in the death of hundreds of citizens. No family was immune to the sorrow of having a loved one die. Margaret Autrey's Aunt Veona Goss was a nurse who died after contracting the flu while caring for patients. The epidemic occurred shortly after the opening of Camp Jackson. When combined with the hundreds that died at Camp Jackson, the area total was over 500.

Hookworms were called the "vampire of the south." They made the victims passive and sapped their energy. On October 18, 1909, *The State* published, "The south cannot close its eyes to the hookworm or ignorance." The article urged curing the affected and using general sanitary precaution. The July 28, 1913 issue called on citizens to eradicate typhoid fever, a preventable disease.

Going to the doctor was not a usual thing before the days of health insurance. Most families relied on home remedies and they hoped the doctor would make a house call if there was an emergency. Margaret recalled that asafetida bags were used to repel germs, quinine cleared up malaria, and castor oil was used for everything else. She said:

> If I caught a cold, my mother rubbed musterole on my chest and put a flannel cloth over it to hold the heat in. And, it was so hot, I complained and complained and finally my mother only used it if she felt that it was a matter of life and death. From the early 1900s through the 1920s mothers concentrated on warding off germs. My mother never subjected me to asafedtida [sic], but the children next door had a stinking bag tied around their necks all of the time. They wore them even before they got sick. Their mother considered it a precaution. They smelled so badly that we thought they would ward off all the germs in the neighborhood. When they came over to my house, their smell would take my breath away.
>
> Vicks Vaporub became popular when I was in elementary school. Mother would put Vicks in a tablespoon and then put a lighted match under it. The Vicks melted and the heated vapor opened my sinuses. Caster oil was everyone's spring tonic. I dreaded it. All the children had to take it, even if they didn't need it. The taste was so awful, my mother tried disguising it in orange juice. I knew better and started making a face before I took a sip.
>
> I didn't have a bicycle, but I had roller skates. I could skate upside down and backwards. So, I got my share of scrapes and scratches. Iodine was the cure-all for wounds. It burned so badly, I dreaded the treatment, even though I was in pain. It didn't stop me from skating.
>
> Hospitals were just getting started when I was born and no one went there unless they were dying. In fact, if we knew anyone who was taken to a hospital, we waited for news of their death. During the early years of hospitals, people were rather superstitious and many people refused to go until it was too late.

Dr. Augustus Baron Knowlton graduated from the Medical College in Charleston and studied in Europe. He returned to Columbia and opened a general hospital on Marion Street in 1900, known as the Knowlton Infirmary. He gained a reputation as an excellent abdominal surgeon. In 1914, the South Carolina Baptist State Convention purchased the infirmary and reorganized it as the Baptist Hospital. It continues to operate on the same property today, although the facilities have been expanded many times.

The United King's Daughters began the first public hospital on May 24, 1892. The largest community project undertaken at the time, it was planned as a center of medical care for all Columbians, regardless of creed, race, or ability to pay. A motion by Mrs. David R. Flenniken began the Columbia Hospital Association. In July of 1892, the city council granted a charter for a 20 bed wooden structure and a 99-year lease on 4 acres of land near the city limits. The initial operating funds of $1,000 were subscribed by women's clubs, charitable organizations, and the city. Additional funds were raised through donation boxes placed in hotels and churches. The cornerstone was laid with Masonic rites on May 3, 1893.

Alexander Talley, B.W. Taylor, T.M. DuBose, and W.M. Lester were among the first doctors on the medical staff of the hospital. Specialists were added and Dr. E.M. Whaley became the first eye, ear, nose, and throat doctor. By 1909, the hospital was debt free and the Columbia Medical Society managed the facility. By 1921, two three-story brick buildings were added in the rear of the original building and the legislative delegation of Richland County appointed a board of trustees to assume the management. The hospital was renovated in 1933 and opened with 275 beds. At the same time, a school for both white and African-American nurses was established.

Cotton prices fell dramatically in the early part of the century. Farmers who recognized the situation attempted to remedy their income by planting twice as much cotton as they had years before. By 1910, 1 acre out of 5 was planted in cotton. Instead of experiencing an increase in income, the market was flooded and the price per pound plummeted. Also, the farmers were further hampered by transportation rates. Railroad freight rates were scaled to send cotton directly to New York rather than to Charleston. It cost three times less to send cotton to northern markets than to Charleston only 90 miles away. The legislature could not solve the problem of over planting; however, a state warehouse system was established. Farmers stored their bales and were allowed to borrow on the receipts.

In 1919, the boll weevil descended on South Carolina and destroyed the entire Sea Island cotton crop. *The State*, February 24, 1991, published a retrospective of the time. In 1920 and 1922, the insect ate its way through the rest of the state's crop. In some areas, cotton production dropped from 37,000 bales to 2,700. It was not unusual for the boll weevil to annihilate 90 percent of the crop.

As the 1920s agricultural depression continued, 50,000 black farmers left South Carolina to seek work in other states. Over all there was very little increase in the population. Banks could not collect their farm notes and 28 failed. Agricultural experts continued to call for the diversification of crops.

Despite the fall of the economy, Columbia in the 1920s developed a lively business as a crossroads area. It was a convenient location for citizens and businessmen within a 30 mile radius. Many merchants developed successful retail stores that stocked a wide variety

The first Columbia Hospital was begun in 1892 from donations from ladies' charitable organizations. It gained financial support from the city, local churches, and other nonprofit organizations.

113

of products. Roads were gradually improved and in 1927 a new Gervais Street bridge took the place of the old rickety wooden floored structure that scared Margaret Autrey to death. "I was terrified to look down as I walked," she said. "The old wooden floor boards were well worn and creaked. When I looked down, I could see the rushing water of the river through the cracks. It was a relief to get a new bridge." The new structure was dedicated as a memorial to the men of Richland and Lexington Counties who served in World War I.

The city government became more efficient when voters approved the election of four councilmen rather than six aldermen. The mayor was to be elected every four years, instead of every year. During these years, women gradually entered the work force. Those who could afford an education worked in clerical positions and as teachers. When the industrial revolution found a place in South Carolina, men, women and children worked in the mills.

The construction of mills in Columbia promised growth—economic and urban. But they also created a chasm of classes. The workers were "all white" yet they were discriminated against. They were called "lint heads" and asked "which side of the tracks they lived on." This new class was part of white supremacy but not white equality. Although every community wanted a mill, the employees were looked upon as cheap labor in a class all by themselves. To many, the mill was a sign of progress. To others, it represented the south developing a northern industry. As northern businessmen invested capital, they went to great lengths to hire local managers to give a totally southern appearance.

The 1881 General Assembly appropriated money to deepen the Columbia Canal, allowing for large textile mills to be built on the river. In December of 1887, the legislature sold the canal to the city. A board of directors oversaw the completion of the project and turned it over to the Columbia Water Power Company.

The Columbia Mill opened in 1894, the Granby Mill opened in 1896, and the Olympia Mill opened in 1904. The new industry attracted people from close-by, rural communities and farms to live and learn skills necessary to produce textiles. Most felt that they had nothing to lose. They felt that staying on the farm meant starvation. A mill job provided one sure thing: cash. The mill quickly became the home of men, women, and children who toiled from dawn to dusk.

Mill sites were selected for the excellent fast flowing rivers as a power source. Available laborers were far less urbane than city dwellers and would work for less money. Locating mills close to the source of the raw material was practical and cut out one transportation cost. Columbia locations provided the bonus of convenient railroad transportation.

The Columbia Duck Mill opened on April 15, 1894 when Arethas Blood, president of Columbia Mills Company, pulled a switch to start the motors. Sewell K. Oliver was the mill manager. His father, Charles K. Oliver of Baltimore, had dug the canal from the penitentiary property to Gervais Street using shovels, picks, and wheelbarrows. He was instrumental in founding the mill. The original design provided for the operation to be powered by a waterwheel at the Columbia Canal, which was west of the building.

The four-story building was constructed mostly of local materials and when completed, contained about 325,000 square feet. Brick from the local Guignard Brick Company was used for the 3-foot brick walls and the timber was provided by W.B. Alderman of Alcolu and Fowles Lumber Company of Columbia. The granite sills for the windows and doors were provided by A.R. Stewart's quarry. It was discovered that the power shafts would not

The electric power house in the foreground was built on the Columbia Canal. The Columbia Duck Mill is in the background. The water from the canal flowed into the plant to generate power for the trolley, lighting for the city, and to run the textile mills.

reach from the wheel to the mill after construction began. The General Electric Company came to the rescue when they proposed the use of electricity as the primary source of power. Until then, the largest induction motor was only 10 horsepower. A hydroelectric plant was constructed on the canal. The General Electric Company developed seventeen 65-horsepower motors for the mill.

The construction was too advanced to alter the building; there was no room on the floor for the large motors. The ultimate solution was to suspend them from the ceiling and have power shafts constructed to run the length of the building. The original motors served the mill until 1927, when the mill switched to commercial electricity.

Since housing for workers was a problem, the company erected a mill village on the New Brookland side of the river called Arethasville. The mill constructed houses for the workers, a school for the children, a park, a recreation complex, and a lyceum hall. They supported the formation of the First Baptist Church of West Columbia. Margaret Autrey's Uncle "B" worked as an accountant for the mill. She was invited to spend many days in the summer and on weekends visiting her cousin, Juanita Goss. She remarked, "We'd rig up in a bathing costume and go to the bath house. We'd go in bathing. We never swam; we just played around in the shallow water."

By World War II, the mill was sold to Mount Vernon Mills, Inc. In 1942, it operated 24 hours a day, 7 days a week making fabric for tents, tarpaulins, hatch covers, boat covers, gun covers, truck covers, collapsible pontoon rafts, stretchers, cots, knapsacks, uniforms, and shoes. The employees supported the war effort: 90 per cent purchased war bonds and the mill received the "T" flag in recognition of their contribution. The mill sold the mill village houses to private owners in 1953. In 1980, the mill closed due to a declining market for duck products. On December 7, 1981, the Mount Vernon Mills, Inc. donated the building to the state to be used as a history museum.

William Burroughs Smith Whaley had a reputation as a mill designer and builder when he came to town and completed the Granby Cotton Mill southwest of town in 1896. Burroughs was known for his innovative designs and built 16 mills in South Carolina between 1893 and 1903. The Granby Mill was the first to operate without power on the site. It was the first major technological improvement in mill design because it drew power from turbines on the Columbia Canal, a mile away. Whaley's success led him to build the Olympia Cotton Mill next to the Granby Mill in 1900. With 110,000 spindles, it was the largest cotton mill in the world.

All mills in the area were in full production by 1900. They contributed to the demise of the small farm while saving the lives of many farmers who faced starvation. Yet the people were no longer self-employed. They had to condition themselves to the rigors of being indoors, having a boss, and standing in one place for long hours . Originally the hands worked 78 hours a week. It was reduced to 60 hours, which meant working 12 hours a day for five days and 6 hours on Saturday. In the early years the pay was about 75¢ per day.

The demand for labor caused Whaley to offer incentives to attract workers. He built a mill village, a community center with a pool, bowling alley, meeting rooms, a baseball field, a park, and a playground. The company store offered the workers credit until payday. Whaley also designed and built the Granby Church in 1900, the south Side Baptist Church in 1901, and the Trinity Episcopal Mission in 1910.

As the mills grew, they were sometimes in conflict with the workers, the local newspaper, and politicians. In the 1900 Labor Day parade, members of the national Union of Textile

The interior of the Olympia Cotton Mills is pictured c. 1900. Drawing frames are in the foreground. Workers were at their jobs 60 hours a week, down from 78 hours a week.

Workers marched double-file down Main Street. They called for reduced working hours and child labor laws. A State Federation was formed and became the largest textile local in the world. The 1901 parade was lead by 80 children who worked in the mills, causing a great deal of public attention. Whaley was not cowed by workers' demands and responded with a lock-out. The movement made few improvements and by December 1901 had run its course.

Whaley sold his mills in 1911 to Parker Cotton Mill Company who made improvements by adding indoor toilets to the workers' homes, curbs, and improved drainage. When Pacific Mills of Lawrence, Massachusetts purchased the operation in 1916, they constructed new houses for the supervisors and managers. The area became known as "silk stocking row."

The uncertainty of crop production, the rise of urban areas, women in the work force, emphasis on education for every citizen, and the impact of technology (industrialization) caused less and less emphasis to be placed on farming. The realities of imminent starvation forced many issues to the forefront. Too many farmers lost or were on the verge of losing their farms. Prices of cotton, tobacco, and produce collapsed. The soil was worn out and loans were only available at usurious rates.

Coleman Blease sprang from Tillman's supporters to become the spokesman for the working class. He didn't dismiss the power of the workingman's vote as Tillman had done. By the time Blease campaigned for governor, the Democrats had to wade through their own factions before they could select a candidate. The party was split three ways—conservatives, progressives, and Bleaseites.

Blease was elected governor in 1910, after two unsuccessful campaigns. When he took office, the public had been in favor of law and order for ten years. They quickly found out that Blease was going to let them down, often in ways worse than Tillman. He fired up prejudices much like Tillman, but he drew the line about class and who should serve the "little man." He won the support of mill workers and those who supported horseracing and gambling. He believed that drinking and gambling were personal matters. Certain factions supported him, including Charlestonians who did not want their racetrack tampered with and owners of drinking and gambling businesses who wanted to keep the status quo.

Protecting immoral institutions revealed Blease's inconsistency when he also claimed to protect family unity and individual dignity. Despite the need for labor laws, he fought regulating safety, wages, public health, and education. He also pardoned a record number of criminals: 1,500. His vetoes included hand written messages using profane language.

During his term from 1911 to 1915, he espoused lynching as "necessary and good." While blacks were his primary target, he also said that he would pardon any man or mob who killed a doctor who had given a physical examination to a young girl. His endorsements frightened most citizens. *The Southern Christian Advocate* printed, "Today the Negro, tomorrow the prominent attorney."

The State campaigned against lynching by printing every detail of an incident and decrying it as murder. This lead to the *Charlotte Observer*'s reference to *The State* as "the sheriff of South Carolina." *The State* also led in the reform of the jury system and laws banning carrying guns. They advocated textile factory inspectors, income tax for the wealthy, welfare work, education for all children. They stopped short of advocating limited working hours. The county option for education finally passed in 1915; however, it was not approved statewide until 1937.

Blease served two terms as governor and therefore stopped reform and progress for four years. He was an embarrassment to the image and prestige of the state, yet he commanded the highest voter turnout in the history of South Carolina elections. In 1910, 80 percent of the voters voted.

At that time, Columbia politicians fell right in step with the example set by the governors. The city commission discontinued holding elections that selected one representative from each ward. All commissioners were elected at large, as a way of keeping out influences and problems facing the local wards. This kept the voices of blacks and mill workers to a minimum. The working class and the African American slowly became neutralized.

The political methods of Hampton, Tillman, and Blease eventually lead to progressivism. When Richard I. Manning was elected governor in 1914, the public welcomed his brand of progress. Blease vowed that Manning would never succeed him. He used red ink to resign rather than relinquish the office to a man "whose philosophy I despise." Lieutenant Governor Charles A. Smith turned the office over to Manning.

Governor Manning championed the modernization of the State Hospital for the mentally ill. He advocated compulsory school attendance and public health education. He supported practicing humane treatment for prisoners. He established the State Highway Department and the South Carolina Tax Commission. He instituted proper revenue management and created enough funds for the support and creation of reforms for 20 years into the future.

He headed the war effort during World War I and backed President Woodrow Wilson's commitment. Former governor Coleman Blease was irate and said, "Dick Manning is the worst governor the state ever had, worse than Scott, Chamberlain, or Moses, because they only wanted to steal your money, and he is trying to steal the souls and bodies of your boys." Neverthless, South Carolina backed the war; thousands served and fund drives raised over $100 million.

By the turn of the century, there were no paved roads in the city. Roads connecting Columbia to other sections of the state were impassable in inclement weather, even though most of the vehicles were still horses, mules, or oxen drawn conveyances. Rain created mud that dried into deep ruts and dust in dry weather. The dirt was insufferable. The streetcar system was the main public transportation for city dwellers. As cars took to the narrow paths and roads, there was much bantering in the press concerning the need for pavement. The editor of the *Columbia Record* stated, "The roads of this state resemble the condition described in the first chapter of Genesis, 'without form and void.' " Taking any vehicle, including a horse-drawn buggy, past the city limits was like launching an expedition. The roads through swamps and traversing streams were always in ill repair. In the summer, crossing the roads in the sand hills involved mountains of hot sand up and down.

In 1899, N.G. Gonzales advocated that brick crossings be built on Main Street to replace the granite stepping-stones. He described the street as "a wretched country road." Until that time, the only improvements had been made between 1894 and 1898 when Mayor William M. Sloan had 115 pedestrian crossings constructed.

With a population of 22,000 in 1902, Columbians were ready for a century of progress. There were 6 hotels, 20 drugstores, 39 doctors, 10 dentists, 6 colleges, 23 blacksmiths,

Governor Richard I. Manning began an era of progressivism in 1914. His six sons served in World War I. At the time this photograph was made, five sons were serving. One son was killed during the conflict.

71 boardinghouses, 28 barbershops, 5 liquor stores, 13 dressmakers, 3 steam laundries, 4 Chinese laundries, 22 fruit stands, 18 restaurants, 31 African-American lunchrooms, 9 stables, and 21 shoemakers. James L. Tapp built a modern department store with the best show windows in town in 1903. There was a city wide streetcar system and railroad tracks radiating in all directions. Yet roads could not accommodate a horse and wagon; the population of rural communities was stranded. Each county was responsible for constructing roads. To save money, most counties used a mixture of sand and clay laid on top of a cleared path. It created thick, oozing mud with the first rain.

On June 4, 1900, Columbians saw their first automobile drive down Main Street. In its June 5 issue, *The State* relegated the news to the second page and covered it in a very short article as cars were no big deal. They were thought to be a fad. In *Old and New Columbia*, J.F. Williams recalled that the first automobile to haul passengers was purchased by Ely Richards and Charles Miller. They planned to run a passenger service from Columbia to Camden. Their idea was shelved after one trip because they ran over a lady on North Main Street, causing the first automobile casualty in the city.

In 1902, Alexander Mason Gibbes bought the business that was begun in 1882 by his brother Wade Hampton Gibbes, Jr., and then sold to their father Wade Hampton Gibbes, Sr. Gibbes Machinery became the Chalmers dealer in 1908 and sold 1,500 in six years. Gibbes got permission to drive a new $550 Maxwell up the State House steps in 1909. It made it up two flights, and the stunt received publicity in *The State*, which contributed greatly to the sales of the vehicle. Gibbes also sold Packard, Peerless, Saxon, Hudson, Chevrolet, and Hupmobiles. The 1904 Oldsmobile Model 6C was built between 1901 and

1906. The company advertised that "the southern tread" fit the ruts made by cotton and tobacco wagons. (The wheels were set 60 inches apart instead of 55 inches.)

Robert T. Clark was an established grocer when he took a chance and opened Central Chevrolet and hired 15 employees to sell and service Chevrolets. He and R.E. Ebert ran a grocery store in Shandon and also a general store near the Pacific Mills. Ebert went on to develop Winn-Dixie Stores while Clark opened on Sumter Street. In 1929, Clark needed more space and opened one of the first car showrooms in Columbia on Hampton Street. He had to tear down a livery stable to make way for a service department. At the time, a Chevrolet sold for $460 and the only color choices were black and green. The body was mostly made of wood except for a thin layer of metal. The only accessories were a rear bumper, a spare tire, and a radiator cap with a thermometer to indicate if the car was overheating. Chevrolets became popular because of the easy handling with a manual shift.

Cars were a menace by 1905; traffic jams and frustrated drivers were commonplace. The speed limit was set at 15 miles per hour on the street, 6 miles per hour at intersections, on hills, bridges, and any places deemed to be hazardous. Even though there had been Good Roads Campaigns in many states, South Carolina did not get on the bandwagon in support of automobiles as a serious mode of transportation until there was an overwhelming demand for services. Despite the growing number of automobiles and the cry from *The State* to build roads, Columbia did not begin street improvements until 1908, when 16 blocks on Main Street were paved from the Union Train Station to Elmwood Avenue. Planners miscalculated when they used a bitulithic material. In hot weather, carriage and cart wheels left impressions on the surface of the roadway.

In an effort to correct the problem, wooden blocks were used to cover Washington and Hampton Streets from Assembly to Sumter in 1911. For years, the blocks swelled and popped after heavy rains if they were not totally washed away. This created unsafe conditions with loose blocks and holes in the road. Bicycle riders avoided the area as the uneven surface caused many accidents. The conditions were not corrected until 1925, when all of the wood was taken up and replaced with asphalt paving. Margaret Autrey remembers when cobblestones paved Gervais Street from the State House to the river.

President William Howard Taft visited Columbia on November 6, 1909, the first president to visit the area in 100 years since George Washington had come. The President lunched at the State House, addressed students at the university, and delivered a speech at the State Fairgrounds. A ride around the city in Edwin W. Robertson's automobile completed his day. Robertson owned the finest car in the area and lent it for the Taft's visit.

By 1910, there were nearly 3,000 automobiles in the state, yet there was no highway department. The first year of the inspection and testing of gasoline was 1913. The State Highway Department was established on February 20, 1917 as a result of years of citizen outcry. In 1920, there were still only 26 miles of roads in the Columbia area. Some were still unpaved and all were unmarked. It was hard for the politicians to see a need to construct roads and improve old roads. It very slowly dawned on them that cars and trucks were practical transportation that would replace trains. Most didn't see this until 20 years after the invention of airplanes.

Zan Heyward, son of Governor Duncan Clinch Heyward, told about a trip to Newberry in his book *Things I Remember:*

> The road . . . was unpaved and wagons and buggies had cut deep ruts in its surface, especially where it meandered through long stretches of sticky red clay. In rainy weather, the road was practically impassable for automobiles with their narrow "pneumatic" tires. Slipping, sliding, and skidding, you usually ended up in a ditch—or bogged down to the axle in the red clay mud. . . .
>
> To even contemplate a trip from Columbia . . . required hours of planning, and checking your car for mechanical defects. On this trip, my Model T Ford was in perfect condition, or so I thought. . . . With my fingers crossed, I started hopefully and prayerfully toward Newberry. Except for the jumping and jolting from rut to rut, everything went well for the first twenty miles. Then, the motor began to sputter and falter. Pulling on the choke helped a bit—for a jerky-jumpy yard or two—until . . . the motor went dead.
>
> In those days, the gasoline tanks were suspended just under the rear end of the car and held in place by wide bands of steel. As I went to the back of the car, one look told me that there would be no need to measure my gas supply. The whole tank was missing.

In 1909, President Taft became the first U.S. President since George Washington to visit Columbia. Flags were flown from buildings and thousands of citizens turned out to cheer the President.

121

An hours wait, and, beyond a curve in the road, I heard the approach of wagon wheels. Then . . . a farmer came with a wagon load of hay and, perched on top of the hay, was my missing gas tank.

Columbia installed its first traffic light in 1922 at Sumter and Hampton Streets. It was a gas light with repeating amber flashes. *The State* newspaper reported that one resident protested that it was an "infringement on his personal liberty." Turn signals were then attached to poles in the center of intersections. Many motorists took no notice; they knocked them down through inattentive driving. Finally, electric lights were set in concrete bases in the middle of the street. This still did little to deter drivers. After a multitude of accidents, signals were hung from overhead wires.

When Margaret Autrey was young, traffic began to build. There were still few cars, but the lack of auto laws created many careless drivers. About 1922, numbers of individual automobiles dubbed "jitneys" cruised up and down the streets seeking riders. For a 10¢ fee a passenger could catch a ride to his next destination. When prohibition became a federal law, some jitneys were known to have delivered special orders to thirsty patrons. When city ordinances imposed fees for licenses and began enforcing traffic regulations, jitneys faded from the scene and gave way to other forms of transportation.

Theodore Autrey purchased his first car about 1924 to allow the family to visit relatives in Edgefield and Lexington more often. Margaret was thrilled to go for rides even though it was a two-seater and she generally had to sit on her mother's lap. It rained the night before their first journey to Lexington, yet everything ran smoothly until they were out of Columbia. Margaret said:

By 1922, congestion and unruly drivers presented a problem. The first traffic light was installed amidst much controversy.

122

We drove for what seemed hours on a dinky two lane dirt road with my mother questioning my father over and over to be sure that he knew where he was going. There were very few road signs in those days and we drove for at least ten miles through open land and woods without ever seeing a person, or a house, or a store. Traveling at the speed of 15 or 20 miles per hour made a trip of ten miles seem like an eternity.

Finally, we made it to within a few miles of Lexington and were confronted with a big hill of slick clay. It looked as though it was slick from the rain and slick from other cars attempting to go up. As I sat perched on my mother's lap, I was terrified of what might happen as my father went into low gear and took a run at that hill. About half way up, the car would not climb any more and we started sliding backwards and then sideways. Mother was yelling, "Theo!" and holding on to me. I held on to the door for dear life, because by then I only had a precarious perch on my mother's knees. It was lucky for us that my father was level headed and calm. The second try he took a more determined run at the hill and made it to the top. My mother and I did not want to travel very far by car after that. After a few more trips, my father realized we were just plain city people and we could walk to all of the places we needed to go or we could catch the train. He sold the car a few years later and we were glad.

The city appointed a commission on waterworks in 1903 with Dr. J.W. Babcock as chairman. The commission developed a new waterworks powered by a waterwheel to pump water from the canal for treatment. It was completed in January 1907; parts of the original plant are still in use. The transformers for powering the plant's high service pumps were installed in 1906. Pump houses were constructed on the canal levee and used to pump up to 7 million gallons of water a day from the Broad and Saluda Rivers, seeming to provide Columbians with a limitless supply of water. A laboratory and control building constructed in 1913 were used until the 1970s.

Irwin Park was designed by John Irwin, the chief engineer of the waterworks and was built at the Columbia Waterworks in 1913. It featured swans in ponds, a zoo, and a gun from the battleship *Maine*. Margaret Autrey walked to the park on many occasions when she was a young teenager. She said:

It was a long way to walk, even though we were used to walking everywhere. The streetcar didn't go there so I was excited to go when invited by people from our church who had a car. We also had a lot of fun going up on Arsenal Hill and walking down the path toward the old ice plant. We also rode the streetcar to the end of the line and back when we had a dime to spare.

When the 20-story "skyscraper" was constructed in 1903 for the National Loan and Exchange Bank Building, citizens were so proud they felt they had one of the wonders of the world in their city. The skyscraper put the city on the map, as very few cities outside of the north had undertaken such construction. The steel framed 12-story red brick building is still standing on the corner of Main and Washington Streets and is best known as the

Barringer Building. Edwin Wales Robertson was president of the bank at the time of the construction. It was beautifully design with molded and decorated stone on the upper and lower levels. An elaborate cantilevered cornice encircled the roof, but was removed in 1965, when it was thought to be hazardous. The building was such a distinct landmark that people from miles around came to see it and to ride up and down on the elevators. For years citizens included references to the skyscraper in casual conversation by saying, "Oh, I work three blocks from the skyscraper." The Barringer family purchased the property in 1953, and the name changed to the Barringer Building.

Margaret Autrey recalled:

> When my cousins came for a visit from Aiken, Augusta, or West Columbia, our favorite activity was to go on top of the "skyscraper" and look down. We went there every chance we got. When I got a camera, I asked the elevator operator to take our picture. The photos marked our trip as a special occasion. The building was a symbol of community pride. I'd see my neighbors taking visitors to see the building and ride the elevator. When I look back, I recall that many people just gawked. We thought Columbia was equal to New York City.
>
> Before my father bought a radio, he'd go down to the newspaper building on Main about a block from the State House. They'd post news bulletins and sometimes they'd print an Extra edition. At night, as the returns came in the newspaper publisher would project the results on a large sign on the building across the street. Thousands of people would stand out in the middle of the street eager to find out who had won. Eventually, we owned an Atwater Kent with a horn on top. Our neighbors might come over when we listened to "Lum and Abner" and "Amos and Andy."
>
> We were teenagers before we'd venture more than a few blocks from home. The big deal in the late '20s and early '30s was a trip to the locks. We'd get a group of friends together and if someone had the use of a car we'd stop at the locks, explore the old area, sit around and talk, have a good time taking pictures, and of course, the highlight of the outing was walking across the old stones.

The Palmetto Building was constructed as the city's second skyscraper. It was located on the corner of Main and Washington, which was the busiest corner of the city. At 15 stories, it was taller than the National Loan and Exchange Bank Building, yet the Exchange Building continued to be known as the skyscraper. The white structure was often referred to as the "Woolworth Building of the South." When it opened in 1913, citizens were impressed with its exterior of interlacing arches, moldings, and cornices. The interior featured marble stair cases, three elevators, and brass hardware.

The Columbia Building was constructed right on the heels of the Palmetto Building. The Union National Bank was located two doors north of the streetcar transfer building on the corner of Gervais and Main, across from the State House. When the bank planned for a new modern location, the transfer building was razed to make way for progress. The building continues to be known as the Columbia Building and has retained its modern appearance.

Margaret Autrey asked the elevator operator to shoot this photo as she entertained her cousins. Margaret is center; Miriam Jones of Trenton and Juanita Goss of New Brookland were visiting for the day.

In many ways, Columbians made slow progress into the machine age while clinging to many old ways. During the teens until about 1922, laundry was picked up in horse-drawn conveyances. Many women both African American and white worked as washerwomen. They came on Mondays and took the customers' clothing to their home and then returned them clean later in the week. Those who washed their own clothes and bedding washed in the yard in large cast iron pots and hung the garments on a clothesline to dry.

From 1917 to the 1950s, the State Legislature controlled the state and it also controlled Columbia. It didn't help that the U.S. senior senator from South Carolina was "Cotton Ed Smith." *Time* magazine printed that he was a "conscientious objector to the 20th century." This was the time framed by two wars and the Great Depression. During this era, local government had to react to the state of the state and the nation. The city was swayed by the U.S. military's establishment of a base, the federal help programs resulting from the Depression, the state government's establishment of administrative services, World War II, and the immediate aftermath of change. The pivotal point of all of these great changes began when the United States entered World War I.

8. INDUSTRY AND THE MODERN ERA

When World War I appeared imminent, Edwin Robertson, president of the National Loan and Exchange Bank, traveled to Washington, D.C. in January of 1917 and invited the military to tour Columbia and consider the area for a training site. Robertson and others in the Chamber of Commerce formed a Cantonment Committee to coordinate pledges to purchase a 1,200 acre tract 3-and-a-half miles east of the city limits for use as a military base. Over $50,000 was collected in 45 minutes.

Major Douglas MacArthur announced that Columbia was a possible site for a new army installation, and Robertson's group offered to donate the land to the government. When Major C.E. Kilbourne arrived in 1917 to review the site and it was approved on May 19, 1917 for a field artillery replacement depot. There was a rush to build facilities for officers and enlisted men because the United States declared war on Germany on April 6, 1917.

The new installation, first known as the Sixth Cantonment, was named Camp Jackson in honor of President Andrew Jackson, a native South Carolinian. Hardaway Construction Company of Columbia won the contract to build the facility. Construction began with 17 carpenters on June 21, 1917. The work quickly escalated and by the middle of July 1917 workers were employed.

At first, the newly cleared site was a tent city. By December 22, 1917, the contractor had completed 1,519 buildings, including barracks, officers quarters, kitchens, stores, warehouses, stables, and entertainment facilities. In addition, there was an airfield, a railroad, a sewage plant, bridges, and roads. Construction was completed in eight months. One hundred electric streetcars were put in operation from Columbia to the military base. The demand for transportation during the construction of Camp Jackson caused an additional 20 miles of rails to be laid. In 1918 alone, 10,805,950 passengers rode the trolley cars.

Within 11 days of establishing the site for the camp, 110 men arrived to serve as guards. The first 8,000 recruits reported for duty in late August and September 1917. By then, the work force numbered 10,000 men, who lived and worked at the site. The 81st "Wildcat" Division was the first to be organized and trained at the Camp by the commander, Major General Charles H. Barth.

A year later, in 1918, 45,000 men were in training. The Red Cross and Women's Service League worked for the welfare of the soldiers, and for the first time women of different backgrounds came together. The Community Club served meals. Private homes were opened to provide rooms and meals when needed. Thousands of khaki-clad soldiers were on the streets. At various times, the population of soldiers at the camp doubled the number of Columbia citizens. Camp Jackson became the home of a mounted band and of the 102nd Cavalry.

When the Armistice was signed on November 11, 1918, the 30th Division was inactivated and plans for expansion were discontinued. Approximately a half million men received training at Camp Jackson and most went overseas to join the American Expeditionary Forces. The 5th Infantry Division trained at Camp Jackson until plans for further expansion were dropped. The facility was inactivated in 1921. From 1925 until 1939, the camp reverted to the Cantonment Lands Commission. The South Carolina National Guard used the property in the summer and on some weekends.

Camp Jackson introduced the outside world to the citizens of Columbia during World War I. Automobiles became popular and businesses grew to sell and service them. The local government became aware of the need to attract businesses and it became necessary to get the word out about Columbia's assets. In 1923, A Boost South Carolina Conference was held in Columbia and the theme of "Wonderful Iodine State" was conceived. These became the call letters of WIS radio station. In 1925, the Columbia Chamber of Commerce got on the boosterism bandwagon and launched an aggressive campaign to attract new businesses and industries to Columbia. They published a book entitled *Columbia Unlimited*, featuring highlights of the city's history, climate, water, and sources for raw materials.

World War I generated large profits for Columbia's mills and attracted northern investors to the area. When profits fell, owners assigned the workers almost double duty with no additional pay. Unrest followed and led to strikes. In 1929, the legislature determined that poor living conditions in the company owned mill villages acerbated the situation.

Camp Jackson was opened to train troops for World War I. Between 1918 and 1939, the army base was only used to train reservists in the summer.

Flying machines first came to Columbia in the mid 1920s when daring barnstorming pilots took off and landed in open fields off Rosewood Drive. There were daredevils willing to fly low down city streets and several flew under the Gervais Street Bridge. Local air shows featured acrobatic pilots wowing crowds of people. Fliers towed banners over the city to advertise, "See Columbia from the Air for $3.00." Paul Redfern was the first to construct an airfield outside of the city limits on Devine Street where Dreher High School now stands. He was one of the first local pilots and mostly used the field for his own purposes. Unfortunately, he was lost while attempting to fly to Brazil in 1927.

Columbia officially opened an airport south of Rosewood Drive in 1929 and named it for mayor Dr. L.B. Owens. Louise Owens LaRoche, the mayor's daughter, christened the first airplane the "City of Columbia" on September 20. The ceremony marked the beginning of regularly scheduled passenger service by Eastern Air Express between New York City and Miami. Airmail service began in 1930. The South Carolina Aeronautics Commission was established in 1935 to give assistance to cities and counties in constructing local airports.

The day the stock market crashed, October 24, 1929, was also Big Thursday. Fourteen thousand fans crowded into the wooden stadium at Melton Field to see Clemson beat Carolina 21–14. It was the next day before the citizens of Columbia grasped what had really happened. Most felt the Depression was not going to be anything more than another recession like the others they had experienced since 1922. Because the city was a center of city, county, and state government, the citizens did not suffer greatly until 1930. As incomes fell and jobs were lost, many people resigned themselves to years of poverty.

The Great Depression affected the entire population of the city. A meal at the Friendly Cafeteria was 35¢ and a steak dinner in a Main Street restaurant was 50¢. Starting pay for workers was $12 a week. Farmers outside of the city limits suffered, and mill orders shrank. Furthermore, there were serious problems to solve, including bootlegging and the enforcement of the state's blue laws.

On December 31, 1931, People's State Bank closed. Unfortunately, the legislature waited until 1937 before helping its citizens. Too many politicians were opponents of social issues, and social legislation was difficult to pass. In Richland County, unemployment was 44 percent and 100 people lived in the city dump behind Elmwood Cemetery. In 1932, 700,000 free meals were served in Columbia.

Blue Laws were passed to keep Sunday as a day of religion. The first one was passed in 1885 and another in 1932. A dollar fine was levied against those aged 15 and over accomplishing any worldly labor, business, or work of their ordinary callings upon the "Lord's Day." While John G. Richards was governor, he rigidly extended the laws to include banning the sale of soft drink. With or without the laws, drinking, dancing, partying, smoking, and breaking the Sabbath were frowned upon. With religion so well established in town, it behooved the citizens to align with a faith of their choice. In the 1920s, everyone in the city knew everyone else. It was obvious who played hooky from church.

The Autreys were members of the Associate Reformed Presbyterian Centennial Church. Margaret said:

> My father "held up a pillar" in the church and was very strict. We walked to
> church every Sunday. I can't remember not going. I loved going there. The

library was nice and I enjoyed going early so that I could read. On Sunday, the children had to be seen and not heard. After church, we were to relax, speak softly, and stay close to home. My father would approve quiet neighborhood walks with friends. Nothing rowdy or energetic was allowed. There was no dancing, smoking, swearing, or card playing allowed—at any time.

The farmer's market located in the center of Assembly Street was two blocks of sheds divided into individual stalls for farmers. Several stores and a bakery were constructed at the end of the market. Margaret Autrey noted:

We were in and out of the market as we needed food, especially fresh produce. On Saturdays the area was crowded with people who came to visit friends as much as for shopping. Mr. Zusman had a location in the market. He did his baking at his main store on Main Street and then delivered fresh bread, rolls, and buns to the market. He also made gluten-free bread for people with allergies. My aunt, Mildred Goss, moved from Georgia and worked at Mr. Zusman's market location part time while she lived with relatives. Most of our food was purchased from a grocery store near our house. Mother called the store and told them what she needed and they delivered. Our milk was delivered right to the doorsteps in glass bottles. There was no such thing as pasteurizing and the milk had a layer of cream on the top. We scooped the cream off of the top. I liked it when my mother would whip it into whipped cream. A lot of the time I'd drink the cream right after it was poured off. It was a delicious treat.

The city market was established in the middle of Assembly Street. In 1912, the original old sheds were torn down. New sheds were built as part of the WPA work programs during the Depression.

When Margaret Autrey was a girl, she had a lot of fun going for walks with friends.

> We could walk anywhere. We walked all over town, and we never worried. The large houses on Senate Street were all beautiful. We enjoyed walking up and down the sidewalk and gawking at the beautiful porches, columns, and porticos. We wondered what it would be like to live in a great place. Mrs. Robert W. Gibbes lived in a lovely old house and I often went to visit her. I was sometimes invited for tea. She didn't have children and enjoyed encouraging the arts by entertaining the young people who were members of the Afternoon Music Club. She gave my mother and me tickets to various musicals and she arranged for us to have Chatauqua tickets. It was the high point of my life in 1927.

Margaret saw silent movies until she was 12 years old and then attended her first "talkie," *Rio Rita.*

> My daddy took me and I was so impressed I've never forgotten it. I don't remember a thing about the movie because I was so awed at the talking.
> The greatest silent movie was "Wings" with Clara Bow. Her leading man was Buddy Rogers. It was fascinating to see all of the airplanes flying around. Airplanes were not an everyday thing at that time. It was less than ten years after World War I and everyone was still war struck. Crowds of people showed up for that movie. I liked it so much my mother let me buy the book and I remember reading it more than once.
> [Admission to the Rialto was only a nickel, yet Margaret preferred the movies at the Imperial:] The Rialto only showed "shoot 'em ups." I didn't care much for the shooting and yelling. Anyway, anyone who was anyone, went to the Imperial on Main Street, near the corner of Hampton. We'd all catch the Saturday matinee, because it was only ten cents. I loved the serials with Pearl White. She was always involved in a cliff-hanger and we couldn't wait to get there the following Saturday to see what had happened.
> My daddy took me to buy shoes if I needed them, if my mother was working. We would walk over to the Kinard Shoe Store on Main Street. . . . I loved new shoes. My mother was a wonderful seamstress and made me beautiful dresses. Having new shoes made me feel well dressed. When I walked I would look down at my shoes for several days. I guess I just liked seeing what my feet looked like. My daddy said, "Margaret, don't look at your shoes, people will think you've never had any."

Congress established the Federal Emergency Relief Administration in May 1933 and Columbia benefited from work relief. Civilian Construction Corps (CCC) work camps for young men were begun and the state park system was developed. The Works Progress Administration (WPA) employed people to build highways, bridges, and schools. U.S. Senator James F. Byrnes was an avid supporter of President Roosevelt's "New Deal." He coordinated the federal funding that saved Columbia.

Many "New Deal" projects and agencies came to Columbia. Projects to improve and extend the water works and sewer system were carried out. Columbia became a district headquarters of the Federal Farm Credit Administration, and a Veteran's Hospital was established. The University of South Carolina began construction on a municipal stadium at the State Fair Grounds in 1934. Carolina Stadium was the largest such facility in the southeast with a seating capacity of 17,600. The city also received $52,000 to build a shed for the farmer's market on Assembly Street. There were 160 stalls that rented for $6 per month.

WPA grants and loans assisted with the building of the Girls' Industrial School, a Reformatory for Negro Boys, the Home for the Blind, and the State Tuberculosis Sanitarium. As the years went on organizations stepped in to aid the unemployed. The Columbia Community Chest and the Ladies Benevolent Society provided invaluable assistance to those in need despite race or religion. Other institutions received funding for major improvements, including the Confederate Home, the Penitentiary, the State Hospital, and the University of South Carolina. The federal funding brought relief and lifted the burden of unemployment. The James L. Tapp Company completed the largest private Depression-era project undertaken. They razed their 1903 store and opened a modern three-story building on the same site in 1940.

Margaret Autrey married Frank Sims in 1933. She said:

Starting out during the Depression was hard. We were lucky that Frank had a job.

Music and theater were pleasant pastimes in Columbians' lives. Students of Julia Quattlebaum, a popular piano teacher, are pictured on the steps of her North Main Street home following a music competition.

131

We stretched every penny as far as possible. Bread was a nickel a loaf and a quart of milk was 10¢. We ate a lot of vegetables. Farmers would come down the street in a horse drawn dray with fresh vegetables—turnips, beans, and things. Ladies from the farm would walk up and down the street and yell, "Butter beans for sale." Housewives went out into the street and bought directly from the growers.

A visit to the doctor was a dollar and sometimes people could not afford that. The doctor had to live too and he often accepted produce in trade for his services. It was sad to see people selling pencils and apples on the street. The Good Fellows Organization was active in collecting food for those who were hungry—especially at Christmastime. When my son, Frank, was born in 1934 the doctor's fee was $50 and his care to stay in an incubator was $1 a day. Things got a little better for us in 1935 when we rented the second floor of a house on the corner of Richland and Sumter Streets for $17.50 a month. To help make ends meet, we sub-let two of the rooms to another couple for $6 a month. Frank worked at the Pontiac dealership and was finding it difficult to make more money, no matter how hard he worked. In 1938, he operated an automobile repair shop on Washington Street until he was stationed at Fort Lee in Virginia during the war.

The largest project in the Columbia area was the building of the Lake Murray Dam. Begun before the Depression, the project helped keep the initial effects away from the city. William Murray and T.C. Williams conceived the privately funded project, located 16 miles northwest of the city, for the sole purpose of delivering adequate electricity to the midlands.

Preparation for construction included acquiring 1,100 tracts of land that totaled 100,000 acres for building a sizeable lake. The process was time consuming and complicated as some of the land had passed down through generations from grants bestowed by King James II of England in the 1700s. Five thousand homes, 3 churches, 6 schools, and 193 graveyards had to be moved. When logging began in 1927, 2,000 men were employed and 37 saw mills were operated. When completed, it was the largest earthen dam in the world and was 1-and-one-fourth miles long, 208 feet high and 25 feet wide. Lake Murray was formed to be 42 miles long with 500 miles of shoreline. State Highway 6 was constructed across the top of the dam to connect Lexington and the Ballentine area. The vision for the project was well ahead of its time and has stood the test of time.

In 1936, the population reached 60,000 and Columbia began to lose the close knit atmosphere where everyone knew everyone. The same year marked the 150th anniversary of the founding of Columbia and it was referred to as the sesquicentennial year. Main Street flourished with blocks of quality specialty and department stores lining both sides of the street. Tapps, Belk, Sylvan's, Copeland's, Marshall's, Caldwell's, Efird's, Haltiwanger's, Kohn's the Cabaniss Shop, and Saxon-Cullum were among the familiar names.

To honor the milestone in the city's history and development, a pageant was produced and historical markers placed throughout the city. The committee presented the University of South Carolina with property to develop an arboretum. A Sesqui-Centennial public park was dedicated. The park features facilities for swimming, camping, and picnicking. Helen Kohn Hennig, chairman of the Sesqui-Centennial Commission's Historical Committee, edited a book entitled *Columbia: Capital City of South Carolina, 1786–1936*.

The James L. Tapp Company completed a major construction project during the Depression. They opened a modern facility on Main and Blanding Streets in 1940.

When Governor Olin D. Johnson took office in 1935, he campaigned for the "little people." He called for a $3 license tag fee and opposed the bond bill. The vehicle license fee of $12 was felt to be too high for the times. He appeared before the legislature and could not get his "pay as you go" proposal passed. He retaliated by declaring the State Highway Department in a state of insurrection and took over, replacing the commissioner with five consultants and an executive manager. He gained the nickname "Machine Gun Olin."

When the South Carolina controller general would not release funds for the governor's proposed highway projects, the governor appointed agents to seize the Highway Department bank accounts. They were turned away as being unauthorized. Johnson called out the National Guard and approached the legislature about control of the Highway Department's projects. The governor lost his battle in court.

The Highway Department debacle weakened the office of the governor and advanced the legislative dominance of the state. In 1936, the General Assembly took away the governor's authority to appoint highway commissioners. They assigned the state treasurer to sign highway bond bills. Two strong leaders emerged that affected the city, the county, and the state until 1973. Solomon Blatt served as speaker of the House of Representatives most of the years between 1937 and 1973. Edgar A. Brown led the Senate from 1929 until 1973. The two were the state government in the 1930s–1960s. It was nearly impossible for a bill to pass without their approval.

Alterations to the State House were undertaken in 1937. The gallery at the west end of the hall of the House of Representatives was removed. Seven rooms were built in its place and a balcony was added. A large mahogany rostrum was constructed and the metal ceiling was replaced by plaster. The shutters from 1880 were removed and Venetian blinds were added. The major alterations made in the ten years between 1959 and 1969 altered the historic appearance. Air-conditioning and a sprinkler system were installed. Carpeting was placed over the marble floors except in the ground floor corridors. Ceilings were dropped,

The Highway Department was often the center of dispute between the legislature and the governor. The department eventually came under the total control of the politicians and weakened the office of governor.

walls were removed, and walnut wainscots were added. The window and door surrounds were changed and other visual changes were created through redecorating.

The Depression adversely affected the economy but not the spirit of southern hospitality. Of greater concern was the exodus of citizens to other areas of the country. By 1939, 80 percent of the states' male college graduates left. By World War II, one-fourth of 2.2 million people born in the state had moved elsewhere. Those who lived in Columbia prior to 1941 followed many traditions of home, neighbors, family, faith, and hard work. The city was a lovely, peaceful pedestrian place where everybody knew everybody. Margaret Autrey recalled:

> People strolled their neighborhood, walking up and down the sidewalks, talking to neighbors, visiting gardens, and swapping plants. Everyone lived with walking distance of Main Street where they could shop or just window shop. My brother-in-law Otis Sims and his wife Laura moved into Shandon that was way out in the suburbs at that time. Their neighborhood was pedestrian. They had a corner grocery store they could walk to. Laura was a plant enthusiast and specialized growing iris. Many people toured her garden in the spring and it got so large she was able to sell plants.

Camp Jackson was reactivated in 1939, two months after the war broke out between Germany and Great Britain. The military activities immediately eliminated the Depression in Columbia. In 1940, the camp began a long-term extensive renovation and military build-up. The base was renamed Fort Jackson; dilapidated, left over structures were torn down and the facility was transformed into a permanent army training center. The activity at the fort was a welcome boost to the local economy; however, it did not prepare Columbians for December 7, 1941.

9. IMPACT OF WAR

Everyone remembered where they were when they heard that the Japanese had bombed Pearl Harbor and once again the realities of war landed on the doorsteps of the citizens of Columbia. The military build-up at Fort Jackson was accelerated as tens of thousands of troops were processed for combat training. The "Old Hickory" Division was one of the first units to reorganize. The fort acquired 53,000 additional acres of land, and four firing ranges were erected. Even though horses were used until 1943, 100 miles of roads were paved. The roads were named to honor Revolutionary War and Civil War figures.

Among the illustrious visitors to Fort Jackson was Winston Churchill, Prime Minister of England. He made a top secret visit on June 24,1942, to be briefed on American air lift capabilities and to inspect the troops. The editors of *The State* and *The Columbia Record* newspapers were among the four local people invited to be a part of the historic occasion. All of the participants were sworn to secrecy, and the story did not break until after Churchill was safely in England.

Even though thousands of South Carolinians joined the military, many were rejected because of illiteracy, both black and white. It was the first time that state leaders realized many citizens could not read. Farms and factories suffered as more and more men were inducted. There was a shortage of labor; however, men not drafted often left their farms for the "sure pay" offered by the textile mills. As the economy was boosted, thousands of new citizens were lured to the midlands by both the military base and the mills.

The war effort became everything to everybody. It brought industrialization and full employment. The demand for war goods and the presence of the army kept prewar industry in business with war orders for the front. Textile mills operated in three shifts around the clock. Many women began working for the first time. Those who were already employed moved to better paying jobs. Banks, department stores, and the city police department also hired women. Gas stations hired females to pump gas. Women and children who stayed on the family farms worked longer hours in the fields to make up for lost manpower.

Eventually, the mills became competitive in their efforts to employ women and youth. They stayed in full production and many stayed open 24 hours a day, seven days a week. To combat the effects on the farmers, the state Department of Agriculture made attempts to lift the morale of the farmers by staging events and parades.

On the flip side, the sudden addition of thousands of military men earning a total of $2 million a month had a positive effect on the local economy. There was a down side, though, because the increase in the population and the atmosphere of war led to an increased use of alcohol, prostitution, and gambling. Females referred to as "fly by night" women congregated in the city on Fort Jackson's payday. These activities required Columbia to hire more police officers and the military base doubled their military police patrol.

In all, more than 500,000 men were trained at Fort Jackson, not including officers, support personnel, or civilians who were employed. Therefore, lack of housing presented a critical problem. The shortage was so great that it nearly caused the fort to close in 1940. The supply and demand created price gouging and some workers paid to have a bed to sleep in on a one shift basis as people were rotated to sleep in the same bed. Allen and Benedict Colleges came to the rescue and quartered soldiers in their dorms. The new city public housing project was turned over to house officers. The United State Housing Administration subsidized the building of 5,000 additional housing units. Price gouging continued despite the agency's admonishment to discontinue the practice. This was followed by the Housing Administration threatening to commandeer private homes.

Hundreds of soldiers were a common site on the streets of the city. They came from the fort to enjoy restaurants, stroll the streets, enjoy a movie, attend churches, and participate in activities at a USO club. Seven United Service Organizations were established for enlisted men—five for white soldiers and two for African-American soldiers. The largest facility was the main USO that opened in early 1942 at the intersection of Laurel and Assembly Streets on the ridge above the industrial park. It was a large modern facility and many dances and socials were held there.

Lester Bates, Jr. lived on Marion Street during the war years. His father, Lester Bates, Sr., had moved the family to Columbia and in 1930 started Capital Life and Health Insurance before the younger Bates was born. During his youth, Lester, Jr. recalled that the streets were safe. He often walked barefooted to John Manus's Elite Restaurant on Main Street and took his place on a stool. He said, "My father was in the restaurant every day. When I went in, I sat on a stool and John Manus took my order and charged it to my father's account. During the war, the Elite was full of soldiers. It was fascinating to sit on a stool and watch them come in and out."

In 1941, it became crucial to find property for an adequate airport. Owens Field was too small for wartime purposes, for it had only two short runways and no control tower. The Lexington County Airport was begun after a site was located on Highway 215 near Cayce. Funding was provided by the WPA and the U.S. Army Air Corps. The first projects included the construction of two runways and a military area.

The project was known as Columbia Army Air Base. It was one of two bases in the United States used for B-25 bomber training. Colonel Gilbert T. Collar assumed command and workers were employed around the clock. The runways were widened and a third runway was added. Crews practiced bombing over Lake Murray. Lunch Island in the middle of the lake was one of the targets. The exercises were not without mishap. A number of planes crashed and sank to the bottom of the lake. The population on the base reached 7,800.

Lieutenant Colonel "Jimmy" Doolittle and a volunteer squadron of 80 used the base to prepare for their secret bombing mission of Tokyo. They marked off a runway to the dimensions of an 888-foot aircraft carrier flight deck. They completed their training in Florida and then shipped out from San Francisco. Citizens of Columbia learned of their raid from April 19, 1942 *The State* headlines, which read, "American Bombers Rake Heart of Japanese Empire." The group became known as "Doolittle Raiders." The 23 surviving "Raiders" celebrated the 60th anniversary of the raid in Columbia on April 18, 2002.

Despite the vast employment opportunities in Columbia and the bumper crops produced by the area farmers, rationing was enforced the same as in other parts of the United States. Butter, tea, sugar, chocolate, red meat, shoes, and gasoline were rationed and were often unavailable. Margaret Sims saw signs announcing "one can to a customer" in all of the grocery stores. She said:

> It was important to be a regular customer of merchants, because some held back rationed items for their regulars. Sometimes you had a coupon for an item that you didn't need and you could trade. One of my neighbors traded a ration stamp for shoes with someone for sugar.
>
> I was a regular customer of the James L. Tapp Company. Most of the sales ladies knew me. Since most of the department stores were sold out of items as fast as they came in, I hated to stand in line just to buy a sheet. I'd tell the sales person to charge a certain item to my account and send it to my house.

Signs were also posted urging "Are You Doing All You Can?" and "United We Are Strong. United We Will Win." Saving was considered patriotic. The rubber to make one tire could protect 12 soldiers with gas masks. Margaret continued:

> As the war went on, we became accustomed to doing without or sharing with neighbors. We thought less about keeping up with fashion and more about having the basics. I made most of my clothes and sewed shirts for Frank. We all hated wearing cotton stockings and we were eager to have rayon stockings that we called "silk," even if we had to stand

The scene above looks north on Assembly Street toward Arsenal Hill. The white structure on the left is the USO building, which was new when Frank Sims took the picture on April 7, 1942.

"Are You Doing All You Can?" was just one of the signs posted around Columbia during the World War II years.

in line to buy them. Ladies who didn't have hose drew a line down the back of their legs with an eyebrow pencil to look like a seam, rather then wear ugly thick cotton hose. I'd crochet baby sacques to make extra money and then drop by Mr. George Brittain's yarn shop and buy yarn to knit sweaters and dresses. Many women went to work and took the place of men who were over seas. In fact, some women did well in jobs that were thought inappropriate or impossible for women. For part of the war, I followed Frank to Camp Lee in Virginia and we rented our house to an officer at Fort Jackson.

Throughout the war years, food prices climbed even though the state Department of Agriculture attempted to maintain price controls. The practice was ironic, since South Carolina was an agricultural state. A pound of bacon before the war was 28¢. By the end of the war, it was 40¢. Fifteen pounds of potatoes went from 4¢ to 6¢, and a dozen eggs went from 33¢ to 52¢.

Some local businesses suffered. Car production was halted so that raw material could be diverted to the war effort. When Robert T. Clarke of Central Chevrolet learned that production would not resume quickly, he shopped throughout the state and bought as many new cars as he could find. He stored them in a steel building at the State Fairgrounds. After they were sold, he was forced to reduce his staff to 35 employees. His business survived by offering automobile service.

There were special war drives in Columbia. In addition to war bond rallies, residents gathered over 80,000 pounds of clothing to send to Russia. Columbia High School students raised $30,000 by selling war stamps—enough to purchase 25 Jeeps. There were scrap metal drives and food drives. Like most citizens, Margaret and Frank Sims grew vegetables in a "victory garden." Margaret recalled, "We had a big backyard and a nice garden; however, even people in town planted a small plot. Everyone was proud to do everything they could do to help win the war."

On Wednesday, August 15, 1945, *The State* headlines screamed, "World War Ends—Japs Accept Allied Terms: Unconditional Surrender." The paper reported that Main Street broke into a din of noise: "It was bedlam with crowds of GIs and civilians pushing up and down the sidewalks and the streets filled with a nondescript parade of cars with horns, bells and backfires reminiscent of the Armistice of 1918. V-E day passed quietly—not so V-J day."

Margaret Autrey Sims and Frank were there:

> It was really exciting! Everyone was downtown. Frank and I were in the parade of cars lined down Main Street. We heard the news and headed for town because we knew everybody else would be there too. Main Street was the only place people knew to gather. It was bedlam; people were running up and down the sidewalk and a few were running out to the cars as drivers inched their way forward honking their horns. After that, we went home feeling better than we'd felt in years. When we woke up the next morning we felt like it really was a new day.

Following the war, the air base was deactivated. Albert L. Wardlaw, president of the Columbia Chamber of Commerce, proposed expanding air service by developing modern facilities at the Columbia Army Air Base. City officials balked at the idea because they could not visualize getting a return on such an investment. Gradually the size of aircraft increased and a larger airport became necessary. Owens Field had no room for expansion and the old Army Air Base with longer runways and thousands of acres for expansion was the best choice for a commercial airport. Owens Field continued to service private planes.

Wardlaw was selected as chairman of the airport commission. In 1947, the Lexington County Airport began operation, although there were no amenities for travelers. Business began in a new two-story wooden passenger terminal; however, the building burned and a hangar was used until 1950 when another terminal was constructed. During this period it was known as Capital Airport.

World War II brought tremendous changes to Columbia. A variety of industry was attracted to the area just as the emphasis on cotton warehousing and exporting faded. It brought full employment to South Carolina and a promising economy to Columbia. During this period, window screens were added to homes and the introduction of air-conditioning led to more business development throughout the city. People flocked to air-conditioned restaurants and movie theaters. In Columbia, businesses opened to provide for the pent up demand for products. Furniture stores, dress shops, men's shops, department stores, and every kind of specialty store was opened—anything that did not resemble a general store.

Columbians abandoned dinner and supper and began to eat lunch and dinner. My mother always said, "Lynn, call your father to supper." The southerners blamed this serious breech with tradition on the influence of Yankees who had married local girls and those who moved back to Columbia after the war. Gradually, local retail stores abandoned the tradition of closing on Wednesday afternoons and began posting regular hours of nine to five, to the relief of many underpaid workers and sales clerks who were used to years of working the hours demanded by the boss six days a week. My grandmother Lilly always referred to those hours as "working from can to can't."

After 1946, Columbians carried 114 years of concern over states' rights on their shoulders. When Franklin D. Roosevelt died, President Harry Truman appointed James F. Byrnes as secretary of state. Despite that, the States Rights party was formed as a reaction to Truman's domestic policies. South Carolina was one of the Southern states who wanted to block his re-nomination. The newly created party elected Governor Strom Thurman as its nominee to oppose Truman.

Columbia changed and grew during the war. Many political offices became elective. More people had the opportunity to serve in government. In September 1949, the city government changed to a council–city manager form of government. Local businessmen, clubs, and the chamber of commerce made efforts to woo northern industrialists to locate sites in the midlands. Success for the state became an important issue. It was important to increase the tax base and to show the world that the city was entering a modern era.

Between 1940 and 1950, the population jumped from 63,300 to 86,900. The increase in citizens combined with the pent up post war needs created a demand for cars, houses, furniture, appliances, and modern goods after 1945. The demand for cars was explosive because General Motors and other manufacturers weren't retooled until 1946. Positive effects from the post war years included the mechanization of farms. It was no longer necessary for planting and harvesting to be done by hand. It became easier to set land aside and plant pine trees.

In 1958, Lester Bates, Sr. was elected mayor. He formed a study group to determine how an airport could be developed to serve Richland and Lexington Counties. In 1962, legislation created the Richland-Lexington Airport District as a subdivision of the state. A governing body was formed with airport commissioners nominated by both the Lexington and Richland Legislative Delegations. There were to be three representatives each from Lexington County, Richland County, and Columbia. The Lexington members felt Columbia would have an unfair advantage. Mayor Bates rectified the situation, agreeing to only one person from Columbia. He selected Wilbur Smith as that member. Lester Bates, Jr. remarked, "My dad thought Wilbur Smith was smarter than any one in the world. Wilbur ably represented Columbia and got all of his points across." A modern terminal building was constructed in 1965 and the Columbia Metropolitan Airport was born.

In 1945, everything was segregated in the same manner as the Tillman legacy. South Carolina faced the result of 55 years of Jim Crow laws. African Americans were discriminated against in every way possible. There were separate entrances, exits, water fountains, and rest rooms. There were signs labeled "COLORED" over doorways, water fountains, and movie theatre balconies. Schools that were supposed to be "separate but equal" were separate but not equal. The legislature established special colleges for African Americans. The situations that laws did not cover were covered by outdated customs. For instance, African Americans were supposed to "know their place."

140

Governor James F. Byrnes was a proponent of segregation, but he was adamant that African Americans have an equal education. He said, "It is our duty to provide for the equality in school facilities. We should do it because it is right." He led what he termed his "educational revolution" and consolidated schools, creating better facilities for all children. To support his plan, the legislature passed a three percent sales tax and disbursed the money to school systems around the state to finance separate but equal schools. His efforts fell by the wayside. On May 17, 1954, the U.S. Supreme Court ruled that "separate but equal" was unconstitutional and illegal. The segregated schools in South Carolina were ordered to immediately desegregate.

South Carolina fought the law in many ways, closing public parks and schools in order to avoid desegregation. Educators, newspaper editors, and college professors who urged legislators and the public at large to comply with the Supreme Court decision were fired. Private Catholic schools moved ahead and were the first to open classes to black students.

Governor George Bell Timmerman took office in 1955 and sought to purge any activist in favor of desegregation from local university faculties. He pressured the State Board of Education to withdraw accreditation for Allen University, causing black students to apply to the all white University of South Carolina. After Timmerman applied the same tactics to the faculty and administration at Benedict College, the Columbia black community rallied and whites who supported the college took a public stance.

In the meantime, the importance of strong leadership came to the forefront when Columbia adopted the council–manager form of government in 1950. This plan allowed

The Doolittle Raiders trained in the Columbia area. The photo above was taken at the Columbia Museum. (Photo by Frank Sims.)

the voters to choose a mayor and four councilmen who in turn appointed a city manager. The council continued to enact all local ordinances and to establish policy. The city manager served as the chief administrator to oversee city operations.

The State newspaper reported that black citizens favored status quo. Yet a serious social revolution began in 1960 when demonstrations began to free African Americans from second class citizenship. Merchants in Columbia were boycotted and marches were organized to protest segregated facilities. Sit-ins were staged at Woolworth's lunch counter following similar demonstrations in Greensboro, North Carolina in February 1960.

Mayor Lester Bates gathered 60 business leaders of both races to discuss racial problems. President John F. Kennedy called Bates and asked him to lead the way to peaceful desegregation. Bates established a secret committee of 28 members to analyze the situation and make recommendations for a solution. Many people volunteered to serve. Lester Bates, Jr. said, "He didn't want volunteers. He felt that they might have an axe to grind and therefore, he chose people from each race that could discuss all facets of an issue. He wanted every point of view represented including extreme opinions."

Mayor Bates particularly wanted chief executive officers, those who were decision makers. He did not accept substitutes. If an executive wanted to send a representative and could not personally serve, the mayor realigned his list. He was ultimately successful and through the committee, eight downtown stores agreed to desegregate their lunch counters on August 21. Other business owners agreed to drop all racial barriers in public places.

Columbia City schools began the admission of black students and all "Colored Only" signs were taken down. Columbia led the way for cities throughout South Carolina to desegregate schools and public facilities. By the gains of organized protest and the efforts of the local NAACP, desegregation came to Columbia very quietly in 1962. The transition was complete when the University of South Carolina admitted three black students, Robert Anderson, Henri Monteith, and James L. Solomon, on September 11, 1963.

Strom Thurmond was elected South Carolina governor in 1946. As a war hero and attorney, he was a natural choice for the job. He is being congratulated by James F. Byrnes, who later became the U.S. secretary of state under President Truman. (Courtesy Clemson University.)

Many shifts in the economy helped to impact changes in government, law and commercial development in Columbia. Among the differences were shifts from agriculture to manufacturing, aggressive economic development, settling of cities and suburbs, and new citizens arriving from rural areas. During the years 1959–1963, Ernest Hollings served as governor. Aside from his positions on desegregation, he discovered that one-third of the work force was illiterate. He went after new industry by observing how other states attracted industry. At the same time, he formulated plans for technical schools to train the personnel that would be needed. Richland Technical College was organized in Columbia in 1962 to train students in technological fields to serve the needs of the midland's industries. In 1974, the college merged with Palmer College and Columbia Technical Education Center to become Midlands Technical College. In 1980, the school became an accredited two-year college and now serves over 20,000 students.

Hollings became well known for carrying a satchel labeled, "Have Satchel Will Travel." He started the ball rolling; between 1959 and 1965, the state accumulated over $1 billion in new and expanding industry. Much of it came to the Columbia area.

The migration of northerners bringing money, ideas, and creativity helped Columbia break away from a rigid political system. It was fortunate for the economy; however, progress eroded many Southern traditions. The 1960s and 1970s began the gradual trend away from regionalism as citizens became more American and less Southern. Thousands of new people from other states developed new neighborhoods and created strong suburbs. The new Republicans became the party of conservatives and the Democrats became liberals. In 1961, Charles Evans Boineau, Jr. became the first Republican to be elected to the South Carolina House of Representatives since 1901.

Senator Strom Thurmond, the South's most famous Democrat, fled the Democratic Party in 1964 and became a Republican even though he had been elected to the office as a Democrat. Shock waves reverberated as many citizens followed Thurmond's lead and shifted their loyalties, even though the numbers of party members didn't greatly increase until the 1970s. Many "dyed in the wool" Democrats defected as the ranks became divisive over issues. For the first time in the state's history, Republicans received more than five percent of the vote, and the state and Columbia embraced a bona fide two party system. Thurmond kept his Senate seat when he ran as a Republican in 1966.

From 1959 to 1965, South Carolina accumulated over $1 billion in new and expanding industry. The State Development Research Center was created in 1964 to provide an economic base study. Governor Donald Russell's four-point program for economic growth encouraged distribution centers, processing centers, home industry, and service supporting industry. He set goals for education and increased employment.

Robert McNair became governor in 1963 and shared some of the success of the Russell administration. He was effective in the development of tourism and envisioned it as a product. He felt that it would eventually have a huge impact on the economy and might prove to be equal to manufacturing. His tourism development plans were successful. This, coupled with the leadership skills and the vision of Mayor Lester Bates, led the way for Columbia to be named an "All-America City" by *Look* Magazine in 1964.

As the capital city, Columbia was anxious to present a positive and progressive image. It was obvious that by doing so its chances of attracting manufacturing would increase. On

143

Strom Thurmond is shown standing on his head. This was taken from a card that he sent to his constituents when he ran for the Senate in 1954. It was sent to Mr. and Mrs. Frank Sloan of Aiken, and their daughter, Frances Sloan Fulmer saved it. (Courtesy Frances Sloan Fulmer private collection.)

Tuesday, February 2, 1965, *The State* newspaper published extensive coverage of the *Richland and Lexington Counties Joint Planning Commission Report*, which was entitled the "Design for Progress." A.C. Flora, chairman of the group, lead the way in the study of the rapid growth of the city and its urban communities. The report provided businessmen, public officials, and residents of the counties with information to help plan and chart future development in an orderly manner. The report recognized the tremendous impact other communities had on the economy of Columbia and used the area extending approximately 8 miles in a radius when using the State House as the center. West Columbia and Cayce fell into the grid. Although they are located in Lexington County, they are only separated from Columbia by the Congaree River. The astounding growth and progress the towns experienced between 1946 and 1960 proved that the towns would be a future growth area.

The report addressed the need for adequate and proper housing and outlined the condition of existing housing in Columbia. Out of the total of 68,677 housing units 76.4 percent were found to be sound, however 15 percent were in a state of deterioration and 8.6 percent were labeled dilapidated. This report spurred a movement to improve housing conditions. There was no mention of historical properties in the report. "Deteriorating" property and "dilapidated housing" were cited as a method of identifying neighborhoods that needed conservation or rehabilitation of unsafe conditions. A campaign was established to halt the "blight" in Columbia.

From post war until the late 1960s, Columbia's downtown was a vital area for shopping even if customers had to drive around the block several times to find a parking place or had to walk three blocks between favorite stores. It was a thriving commercial mecca, and Main Street boasted an impressive array of quality establishments. When Dutch Square was built on Bush River Road, downtown merchants were experiencing two decades of growth. Most managers didn't worry because they felt their customer base would remain loyal. Soon they had to come to terms with shrinking revenues as shoppers discovered free parking and a closed mall offering a controlled environment.

In 1966, the city council began considering ways to keep the downtown area as a vital retail hub. They purchased open-air trams from the New York World's Fair to provide free shuttle service for shoppers. They were named the *Carolina Queen*. The city opened a new parking facility on the corner of Blanding and Assembly—a block from Belk, a block from Berry's On Main, and two blocks from Tapp's.

To stem the tide of suburban flight, Belk, Tapp's, Haltiwanger's, Berry's on Main, and Davidson's promoted fashion and their service of delivering merchandise right to the door of the purchaser or to a gift recipient. Brides-to-be were excited to receive great numbers of gifts when the department store truck arrived. Belk employed Lynn Sims to develop events and programs to attract young customers. The Young Columbia Council teen board began in response to national studies indicating the buying power of teenage baby-boomers. For the first time, merchandise was promoted directly to teens. Each of the area high schools nominated two representatives; the Council presented fashion shows, beauty workshops, and a weekly radio show featuring teen members on WCOS every Saturday morning with Woody Windham and Lynn Sims.

Berry's on Main also provided special sales and presentations. Miriam Ford was the expert wardrobe coordinator and the busiest woman in fashion, as ladies flocked to her to be dressed head-to-toe for every special event. Everyone knew that Joe Berry stocked the best looking clothes in town. His selection of shoes was only second to Proctor's, which sold the "finest shoes in the south." Miriam recalled the late 1960s and early 70s:

> It was a hey day on Main Street. You would have thought it was a gold rush town. People came from all over the state to shop. We had really great stores then, and women shoppers could go from one fashion destination to another. It was a time when customers were concerned about service. They appreciated being waited on, having expert alterations, nice boxes, and a constant flow of new items from which to choose. Joe Berry was a genius. He knew trends before they became trends. I was in New York on a buying trip and Mr. Berry said, "Miriam, go back into the market and buy white suits." After working with Joe for years, I knew not to question him. I went back into the market and bought white suits, even though no one else was buying white suits. I'd hardly gotten back to Columbia, when customers were coming in asking for white suits. It was unbelievable. We were the only store in town with white and they flew out of the door. Mr. Berry's slogan was "If it's new, it's at Berry's On Main."

The downtown "fashion stores" included Belk, Berry's, Lourie's, James L. Tapp Company, 'Lisbeth Wolfe, and Haltiwanger's. They presented their fashion image through radio commercials, television commercials, trunk showings, box lunch presentations, and seasonal fashion shows. Gala events were held at the Wade Hampton Hotel.

By 1966, state government was the biggest business in Columbia, employing one out of five employees. This enriched all businesses, banks, and institutions and brought full circle the original reason Columbia was founded. There remains, however, a small division between Columbia the city and Columbia the state capital. Those who do not work for the state have local interest and their outlook tends to be different from that of the regularly employed citizen.

Many old homes were razed before conscious preservation efforts could be made in the 1960s and 1970s. The Historic Columbia Foundation was established in 1964 to operate and maintain three historic properties. The organization gained support from the Columbia City Council, private donations, and members. Both the Hampton-Preston house and the Ainsley Hall mansion known as the Robert Mills House were rescued by the organization. With the South Carolina Tri-Centennial celebration of 1970 approaching, the Hampton-Preston house was restored to its 1850 appearance. Two geodesic domes providing 20,000 square feet of exhibit space were constructed next to the house and were known as the Midlands Exposition Center. On April 21, 1970, an exhibit of South Carolina history from

Woody Windham was known as "Woody with the Goodies" and the most listened to DJ on radio. He is pictured above with Lynn Sims and Pat Clyburn c. 1968 in the juniors department at Belk Department Store during a remote broadcast.

1770–1870 opened to the public. The house is now on the National Register of Historical Places and open for tours.

The Ainsley Hall family never resided in the new house they constructed and it is now known as the Robert Mills House in honor of the famous architect. It too was rescued from deterioration by the Historic Columbia Foundation. The group also arranged the funding for the reconstruction of two flanking outbuildings. The home's interior was finally completed by Mills' original design. Therefore, the structure begun in 1823 was sold to the Presbyterian Seminary at Hall's death and was not completed as per the original plans until 1967. The house is now authentic and the four main rooms on each floor feature period museum quality furniture and chandeliers. The property is located at its original site surrounded by a 4-acre city square and is open for tours. The foundation also manages the Woodrow Wilson Boyhood Home and the Sims-Mann Cottage. The Wilson house was built in 1872 and the yard still features magnolia trees planted by Mrs. Wilson.

Lester Bates spearheaded much of Columbia's growth during his 12 years in office from 1958 to 1970. In 1965, Columbia received an "All America City" award (based on city planning and race relations) presented by the National Municipal League and *Look* Magazine. During his tenure, Fort Jackson was annexed into the city limits. He helped with a campaign to promote a new liquor law to increase tax revenue. The move was promoted by the Foundation for Modern Liquor Regulation and Controls and the Greater Columbia Chamber of Commerce. There was great opposition from religious organizations, yet the General Assembly let the voters decide if the state constitution should be amended. On November 7, 1972, voters overwhelmingly voted to allow mini bottles instead of brown bagging.

In 1973, Fort Jackson officially became the U.S. Army Training Center. Aside from the thousands of recruits processed and trained at the base, the announcement assured 3,000 civilians of jobs. The fort grew to a city within a city with churches, athletic fields, golf courses, libraries, banks, commissary, and hospital.

The police department became more accessible to the citizens in the 1970s. In 1975, a municipal court building was opened with six courtrooms. Its drive-in window was opened to collect payments of fines 24 hours a day. In 1979, the city was divided into four areas so that the same officers patrolled the same neighborhoods. This was a move to facilitate citizens and merchants getting to know the officers in their neighborhoods. By 1980, the police department had a staff of 263 and was equipped with over 60 vehicles including patrol cars and motorcycles. Helicopters were used for emergencies.

The construction of the Palmetto Center was announced in 1980. The proposal included a 400,000 square foot office building, a 300-room hotel with convention center, and a 1,000-car garage. The original plans included the demolition of the Palmetto Building. The Palmetto Society for Heritage Conservation was organized in the summer of 1980 "for safeguarding Columbia's historic Palmetto building." The members began a battle to save the building and they prevailed. The Palmetto Building stands next to the Palmetto Center in harmony with the environment.

Preservation presented urban dilemmas and progress often made preservation seem impossible. In 1980 and 1981, many serious questions were posed about these issues.

Letters to the editor reflected the frustration of residents over the progress in Columbia. One said, "Look for it in books, it's no more than a dream remembered; a civilization gone with the wind." Other residents questioned, "Where is Columbia?" Some old structures were adapted for modern use. For instance, Laurel Street homes were renovated and turned into professional offices. In October 1982, *The State* newspaper noted that 23 buildings had applied for landmark status.

The status of the historical Columbia High School building brought the questions of renovation and razing to a head. The last class of the school was held in 1975 and then the entire student body was transferred to a new building in the St. Andrews area. The vacant structure was then used for vocational rehabilitation programs.

The sale of the high school building began in 1981 and was the subject of top news stories for local media until 1983. It began and ended as a contest between the Board of Trustees of the Columbia Academy who owned 75 percent of the property and the Richland County School District One Commissioners who owned 25 percent. The other players were the Richland County Public Library, who had an interest in building a new library on the site, and the First Baptist Church, which wanted to build a new sanctuary. Things became more complicated when the Palmetto Society for Heritage Conservation fresh from their success in saving the Palmetto Building joined the fray. The school was already listed on the National Register of Historic Places so it seemed logical that it could be saved. The school administration applied for adaptive reuse of the property as an art center. The library was interested in the location as a site for a new library that would be next door to the existing library. All the while, the church pressed to purchase the property based on a promise from the academy board. Friends of Columbia High School was formed by former students and supporters of preservation with a mission to save the school.

Next, the Columbia Landmarks Commission weighed in. It was created by the city council in 1974 to protect the beauty of the city and improve the quality of the city's environment through preservation and the enhancement of distinctive structures. The commission also determined if demolition permits could be issued for landmarks. The input of the members became pivotal.

The situation turned into a melee when the Greater Columbia Chamber of Commerce, the Downtown Action Council, the State Chamber of Commerce, the State Development Board, Parks and Recreation, Governor Dick Riley's office, and various politicians, preachers, and businessmen all got involved with questions concerning the property.

Despite all of the disagreements, the sale of the property to the First Baptist Church went forward. In November 1982, the preservationists groups filed suit to block the demolition of the school. They lost in court in 1983 and the Baptist Church lost no time in razing the school building to make way for their new 3,000-seat sanctuary. The defeat did not dampen the spirit of the preservationists. There remains a staunch group who wishes to build, rebuild, preserve, and revitalize Columbia. In 1981, the legislature passed a bill allowing for investment tax credits of 15, 20, or 25 percent, depending on whether a structure undergoing remodeling will be used for commercial purposes or as a residence. The tax breaks give developers incentive to reuse old structures.

Preservation has never been a priority during any period in Columbia's history. Most developers feel that buildings stand only as long as the free market lets them. They feel that preservationists should acquire the property at market value and thereby "save it." Additional conflicts arise when property owners want the free use of their own property. Clashes between preservationists, dollar-ready developers, city planners, and politicians wanting to generate tax revenues for the city are perpetual scenarios in Columbia.

The Palmetto Building was reconstructed per the original plans as part of a preservation effort after narrowly avoiding destruction in 1980. It is open to visitors.

10. Impressive Growth

The visions held by the Taylor, Gervais, Blanding, and Hampton families proved fateful for the establishment of Columbia. The idea of a central city for government has carried Columbia from century to century since 1786. Its accessibility at the geographic center of the state has been the secret of its growth. Emphasis on commercial markets, communications, and transportation aided the city's recovery following the Civil War and helped to reestablish it as a commercial center.

In 1986, Columbia celebrated its bicentennial—"Old Columbia and New Columbia Blend." Attention was given to the radical changes accomplished over decades. Ongoing and future projects were emphasized and revitalization projects began non-stop. Much of Columbia's progress during the period was attributed to Kirkman Finlay, mayor until 1986. *The State* newspaper complimented his bold vision and announced that he left a "legacy of progress." Finlay Park was named in his honor and was the result of transforming Seaboard Park. The site of Sidney Park so loved by citizens in antebellum times was revived and returned to the people as a place for community and family gatherings. The spirit of the old was captured anew with a grassy meadow, walking paths, trees, a waterfall, and a pond.

The 1980s were for restoration as well as for new construction. On February 12, 1986, *The State* announced a $45 million expansion that included moving into a new 200,000 square foot building. The investment included state-of-the-art presses and increased the paper's ability to produce printing and high fidelity color. Nine months later, the State-Record Company shocked the community when they sold *The State* and other publications to Knight-Ridder, Incorporated of Miami. The transaction ended almost 100 years of family ownership.

Columbia remains a thriving city of developing industrial and commercial opportunities. However, the gradual flight of businesses and residents to the suburbs in the in 1970s and early 80s presented a challenge to local government, action committees, and the chamber of commerce. Much planning went into attracting an inner-city population to sustain basic services and to provide a base for a thriving community.

City re-population became a serious part of Columbia's urban renewal. It was needed to support the various institutions and to bring life to the inner city. By 1984, stimulating residential growth and saving the downtown area were priorities. By the end of the 1970s, the once pedestrian city covering 400 blocks became a ghost town after 5 p.m. and on weekends. By addressing preservation, new construction, and revitalization issues, new structures were added to the skyline; many old structures were recycled for new purposes. For instance, The James L. Tapp Company, once the most prestigious department store in the city, went out of business. The abandoned store found a new life as modern apartments.

The Columbia Vista project was begun in 1984 as a long-range project. The first question asked was, "Who wants to live within eyesight of the Central Correctional Institute?" The answer was simple: "No one." In 1987, the long-term demolition of the prison complex began and the project is ongoing. During the same period, the city took advantage of the beauty of the canal and river and revived the old Irwin Park site; the Riverfront Park opened in 1984. Visitors enjoy picnicking, fishing, walking, jogging, and bicycling on the 2.5 mile canal path. Future plans include the incorporation of the old prison building into a destination shopping area.

Much of the industrial dilapidation was cleared in the Huger Street area. It is part of the Vista and is being revitalized with modern office buildings, a new hotel, restaurants, parks, and high rise residencies. A 7 acre Memorial Park was built at the top of the hill in 1986 and features the largest Vietnam memorial of its type outside of Washington, D.C. Other memorials include Pearl Harbor, China-Burma-India Campaign, and the U.S.S. *Columbia*.

The urbanization of Columbia now stretches way beyond its original 2-mile square area. In 1936, it included 9 square miles; by 1986, it stretched over 117 square miles and moved outside of the Richland County line. Many citizens in Lexington and Richland Counties commute to work in the city. Over the years, many small suburban communities were

Finlay Park is located on the site of beautiful Sidney Park, which later became the area of the unsightly Seaboard Park. This photograph shows the area now known as the Vista. (Photo by Burke Salsi.)

The Reconstruction structure of the central prison, here seen from Vista Park, is being incorporated into a shopping area as part of the vast urban renewal project. (Photo by Burke Salsi.)

incorporated into the city limits. Citizens formed groups such as the Columbia Council of Neighborhoods, dedicated to increasing the citizens' voices in local governmental decisions. The neighborhoods in the organization include Earlewood, Eau Claire, Elmwood Park, Melrose Heights, the University area, and Yorkshire.

Columbia's tobacco, textiles, and cotton took the city into the twentieth century, but these businesses did not survive to the twenty-first century. The industry that helped to bring about the industrialization and modernization of the city and county ultimately died from the forces of international competition. As textiles were left behind, Columbia turned to service-oriented businesses and the development of regional centers. The city gained new industrial, sales, and technological companies. There was an emphasis on accessibility, enhancement of communications, and transportation. Blue Cross Blue Shield, Policy Management Systems Corporation, Bell South, Louis Rich, and Allied Fibers became the largest employers. However, the South Carolina State government and Fort Jackson remain the key employers.

As economic ambassadors go forth to attract business and industry, Columbia's past and present as a marketing center provide the basis for the area's future. Columbia ranks among the top five cities in the nation in the number of interstate highways intersecting within or near the city limits. Although the original eighteenth-century grid of streets remains the backbone of intercity transportation, ribbons of four lanes and eight lanes interweave the boundaries of the city and bisect many areas of urban development. These major arteries connect business, citizens, travelers, and trucking transportation to every state in the country. Interstate 26 connects Columbia with Asheville and Charleston and defines the bedroom communities of St. Andrews, Whitehall, Irmo, and Harbison. This high-speed corridor began connecting people to their jobs in the 1960s and remains critical for workers who commute from outlying areas.

Columbia connected to Charlotte in the 1980s via Interstate 77 and citizens were relieved from driving the miserable two-lane road that twisted through Fairfield County, Great Falls, Fort Mill, and Rock Hill. When I-77 later connected with I-26 south of the city, it greatly benefited residents of Dentsville and the Fort Jackson areas and attracted a greater number of travelers.

Trains remain an important part of the daily scene, however. For over 100 years, they blocked Gervais Street and were a pain for motorists traveling to and from work from West Columbia. A $30 million investment was made between 1984 and 1988 and the tracks were lowered below street level, allowing a free flow of traffic into the central business district. Trains continue to use the tracks on South Main Street, even though the 1902 Union Station passenger terminal was converted into a restaurant.

Though the old Columbia Mill buildings on the river were deserted, they left a legacy and history. In 1981, they were donated to the state for a state history museum; South Carolina Electric and Gas Company donated land for parking. The building was reconstructed to house exhibits, artifacts, a gift shop, and a few state offices. The Confederate Relic Room moved from the War Memorial Building in September of 2002 and opened in the mills adjacent to the State Museum. Hundreds of artifacts are displayed, including pistols, sabers, scabbards, and rifles from William Glaze's Palmetto Iron Works, General James Chestnut's "red shirt" from the Hampton campaign for governor, and other memorabilia. Construction is underway for a children's museum and future plans include an IMAX theater and a planetarium.

The changes in downtown have been dramatic. Anyone returning to Columbia after a 25 year absence would scarcely recognize the skyline. The Bank of America Tower replaced the Columbia Hotel on the corner of Pendleton and Gervais Streets. The AT&T tower was constructed on the corner of Main and Gervais after the Wade Hampton Hotel was razed. The $45 million structure stood 26 stories tall; at its completion in 1987, it became the tallest building in South Carolina. The Richland County Public Library was eager to move to a new facility in the 1980s. Planners originally had their eye on erecting a facility on the Columbia High School property. When the First Baptist Church purchased the land, a state of the art library was erected on the corner of Assembly and Hampton Streets in 1989.

During this period, most of the retail stores moved from Main Street, As they left, one by one—Rich's, Tapp's, Belk, Kohn's, Haltiwanger's, Berry's On Main, 'Lisbeth Wolfe—there was an increasing urgency to save the city. The development of up-scale inner-city housing, the restoration of old neighborhoods, construction of office buildings, and fostering the arts has created a comeback for the city. The arts rose to major proportions with the construction of the Koger Performing Arts Center on Assembly Street in 1987. It was a joint venture of the city, the county, and the University of South Carolina. Ira M. Koger donated $4 million toward the construction of the facility, which features a 2,300 seat auditorium.

In the summer of 1988, the Columbia Museum of Art moved from its location in the old Thomas Taylor (great grandson of the colonel) house on Senate Street and dedicated a new multi-million dollar facility on the corner of Hampton and Main Streets on the site of Belk's Department Store. The five-story store was partially razed, leaving room to build a lovely public plaza that separates the museum from a high-rise bank building.

Additional arts programs come from The Columbia Symphony, the Columbia Civic Ballet, the Town Theater, the Columbia Museum of Art, the South Carolina Museum, and the McKissick Museum. Colleges and universities also boost culture through fine arts programs, faculty presentations, recitals, readings, and live theater. The Richland County Public Library presents programs for all ages, including an annual children's book festival known as A Baker's Dozen.

The Riverbanks Zoo opened in 1974 and brought with it a vision for using the water on both sides of the river as a special setting. It began with one Royal Bengal tiger named "Happy" and a fund raising campaign known as "Zoo's Who" and the project has grown into a sanctuary for more than 2,000 animals that are cared for in natural habitats. The exhibits include an Aquarium Reptile Complex, a farm, a sea lion pool, and giraffes, zebras, lions, elephants, alligators, and birds. The Riverbanks Botanical Garden is located on the west bank of the Saluda River and joins the zoo by a 700-foot bridge. The garden is set on the site of the old Saluda textile mill. It features three topographic areas, including the flood plain valley, the valley slopes, and the uplands.

Fort Jackson and Columbia worked well through peace times and through every war since World War I. In 1967, Columbia annexed the post into the city limits. The fort, the citizens, and the city continue to work together. The fort trains thousands of new recruits each year, including approximately 48 percent of all soldiers. In 2001, 36,526 men and women passed though for their eight weeks of basic combat training. Those who complete the training are given combat support service assignments when they graduate.

In 1995, the General Assembly approved funding for a major renovation of the State House. It was begun to repair the structure and bring electrical, plumbing, and heating up to code and meet standards for fire safety, handicap accessibility, and earthquake protection. The process began in 1997 and included restoring the building to its original layout and style. The original copper on the dome had oxidized to a deep green color. The new copper sheathing changed the appearance of the dome. Joe Rogers, director of the South Carolina Department of General Services said:

> There was a great deal of consternation over replacing the old copper. It was surprising how many people were distressed by it being new and shiny, rather than old and green. The current atmospheric conditions were analyzed and I was told that it would take about fifteen years for enough oxidation to occur for the copper on the dome to turn green. Of course, that doesn't take into consideration how active the pigeons will be. During the renovation, a few artifacts were found like cannon balls and old Edison light bulbs. We collected them and had them documented.

Today, the ground floor of the state house remains intact, as well as the basic interior plan, the lobby, and the library, and the building is open for tours.

The governor's mansion became part of a complex along with the Caldwell-Boylston House built in 1830 by John Caldwell, president of the South Carolina Railroad. The complex also includes the Lace House, built in 1854 after John Caldwell gave the land to his daughter Mary Caldwell Robertson as a wedding gift. Through the years many efforts have been made to transform the military academy officer's quarters into an elegant home for the governor. In 1907, the legislature appropriated $500 for Governor Martin F. Ansel to redecorate. Gradually the house was used as a site for entertaining visitors, including Presidents Franklin Roosevelt, William Taft, and Dwight Eisenhower. The Governor's Mansion Committee now makes decisions about restoration and in 2001 the commission carried out an extensive renovation.

The Metropolitan Airport has moved passed Lester Bates's vision into an important transportation center for commercial and public transportation. A $50 million upgrade improved the facilities appearance and function in 1997. The terminal features a two-level concourse, a food court, and expanded ticket counters. The entire airport area was boosted in August of 1996 when United Parcel Service opened an $80 million Southeastern Regional hub offering next day, second day, and third day service.

The University of South Carolina has grown from one building on a two-square block campus to 156 buildings on 351 acres. Eight campuses spread through the state boast of

The State House underwent a massive renovation in 1997, which included replacing the original copper on the dome. The new shiny patina has dulled; however, it will not return to the familiar green shade until after years of oxidation. (Photo by Burke Salsi.)

155

37,307 students. The system offers 350 undergraduate and graduate courses. On March 1, 2003, the Strom Thurmond Wellness and Fitness Center opened to students. The 192,000 square foot facility was named to honor Strom Thurmond, who retired from the U.S. Senate at the age of 100 in January of 2003.

The Carolina Stadium was renamed Williams-Brice Stadium to honor university benefactors in the Williams and Brice families and Martha Williams Brice in 1972. Since then it has undergone transformation after transformation in an effort to have enough seats for all of the football loving fans in the state. An upper deck was added on the west side in 1971 and brought the seating capacity to 56,140. An east side upper deck was added in the 1980s and the latest decks on the end zones brought the seating capacity to over 80,000. No matter how large the efforts have been, the stadium is sold out every time Carolina plays a home game.

Columbia is a continuously expanding urban center, yet the feeling of community has not been lost even though state government facilities and the University of South Carolina have grown to gigantic proportions. Likewise, many areas around the city have grown proportionately. The town of Lexington has expanded in large part because of Lake Murray. In the 73 years since the dam was built, recreation has contributed to the growth of resorts, summer homes, and businesses catering to water sports.

In 2002, the business environment of the area was threatened with the announcement that the lake had to be lowered to relieve pressure on the dam so that an additional reinforcement dam could be constructed. The news was bad for businesses dependent on recreation especially since boating would be difficult. It was great news for the citizens of Columbia to know that their water supply and power supply would be protected for years to come. An article in *The State* on March 9, 2003, noted that the draw down shrank the lake from 47,500 to 36,000 acres after 30 percent of its water was removed. The new dam construction was ordered by the federal government as a protection for the midlands residents in case of an earthquake. The low water level will be sustained until the middle of 2004 when the construction is to be completed.

The spirit of the city continues to meld with that of the state. The accomplishments of Columbia well represent local and state interest. As the capital of the state and a showcase city, Columbia will never escape the scrutiny of the South Carolina Legislature. With the state's political power concentrated in Columbia, it is obvious that politicians, pundits, investors, and citizens share a vision of the future. Even out of town politicians are mindful of having Columbia serve as an example for other cities and towns in South Carolina. The ingress and egress of politicians from all over the state will continue to influence Columbia every time the legislature meets—just as it has since 1790.

BIBLIOGRAPHY

Andrews, Judith M., ed. *A History of South Carolina's State House*. Columbia: South Carolina Department of Archives and History, 1994.

Bailey, N. Louise, Mary L. Morgan and Carolyn R. Taylor. *Biographical Directory of the South Carolina Senate. Vol. III, 1776–1985*. Columbia: University of South Carolina, 1986.

Chestnut, Mary. *A Diary of Dixie*. New York: Gramercy Books, 1997.

Ellet, Elizabeth F. *The Women of the American Revolution*. New York: Baker and Scribner, 1848.

Graydon, Nell S. *Tales of Columbia*. Columbia: R.L. Bryan Company, 1964.

Green, Edwin L. *A History of Richland County, Vol. I 1732–1805*. Columbia: University of South Carolina.

Griffin, Frank Sr. *Main Street As It Was Years Ago*. Columbia: Frank Griffin, Sr., 1968.

Heyward, Zan. *Things I Remember*. Columbia: The State-Record Company, 1964.

Henning, Helen Kohn, ed. *Columbia: Capital City of South Carolina, 1786–1936*. Columbia: The Columbia Sesqui-Centennial Commission, 1936; R.L. Bryan Company (with a mid-century supplement), 1966 by Charles E. Lee.

Huff, Archie Vernon Jr. *Tried By Fire*. Columbia: R.L. Bryan Company, 1975

Latimer, S.L. Jr. *The Story of The State and The Gonzales Brothers*. Columbia: The State Printing Company, 1970.

Malone, Dumas. *The Public Life of Thomas Cooper*. New York, 1926.

Maxey, Russell. *The Columbia High School Story, 1915–1975*. Columbia: Crowson-Stone Printing Company, 1984.

————. *Historic Columbia*. Columbia: Historic Columbia Foundation and R.L. Bryan Company, 1980.

Meyer, Jack Allen. *William Glaze and the Palmetto Armory*. Columbia: South Carolina State Museum, 1982 and 1994.

Mills, Robert. *Statistics of South Carolina, A View, of Its Natural, Civil and Military History*. New York: Hurlbut and Lloyd, 1826.

Moore, John Hammond. *Columbia and Richland County, A South Carolina Community, 1740–1990*. Columbia: University of South Carolina, 1993.

Oliphant, Mary C. Simms. *South Carolina Reader*. Columbia: The State Company, 1927.

Pierce, Robert A. *Palmettos and Oaks, A Centennial History of The State*. Columbia: The State Record Company, 1991.

Regulations for the Army of the Confederate States, The Articles of War. New Orleans: Bloomfield and Steel, 1861.

Selby, Julian A. *Memorabilia and Anecdotal Remeniscences of Columbia, S.C.* Columbia: R.L. Bryan Company, 1905.

★Sherman, General W.T., *Memoirs of General W.T. Sherman, Written By Himself, Vol II.* New York: Charles L. Webster Company, 1892.

Simms, William Gilmore. *The Sack and Destruction of Columbia, South Carolina.* Columbia: Power Press of the Daily Phoenix, 1865; reprinted Dahlonega, GA: Crown Rights Book Company, 2000.

Williams, J.F. *Old and New Columbia 1786–1929.* Columbia: Epworth Orphanage Press, 1929.

Wright, Louise Wigfall. *A Southern Girl in '61, Diary of a Confederate Senator's Daughter.* Gansevoort, NY: Corner House Historical Publications, Reprinted 1999.

★Author's note: Mr. and Mrs. Tolbert Bissell of Greensboro, North Carolina, generously allowed the use of Henry Taylor Williams' (grandson of Col. Thomas Taylor and grandfather of Mr. Bissell) personal copy of Sherman's memoirs. He purchased the volume February 1898 and penned the following inscription on the inside cover: "I have bought this volume that I may learn from his own words, what manner of man he was. (Signed) Henry T. Williams."

NEWSPAPERS, PRINTED MATERIAL, AND INTERNET:
Campbell, Mike. "Cayce Descendant Recalls Historic Family Home." *The Journal* June 11, 1975.

The Carolina Telegraph, 1817.

The Columbia Gazette, 1794.

The Columbia Record.

The Columbia Telescope, 1831–1839.

Columbia Unlimited, Columbia Chamber of Commerce publication, 1925.

The Daily South Carolinian, Columbia, January 18, 1862.

The Daily Southern Guardian, Columbia, December 13, 1861.

Granby Mill Village Historical Survey Report, project of the South Carolina Department of Archives and History and the City of Columbia, 1990.

The Greater Columbia Magazine, Vol. 1, No. 4, July 1977.

Harper's Weekly.

The New Bern Journal, 1903.

The Phoenix.

Southern Times and State Gazette

The State.

www.yale.edu—The South Carolina Ordinance of Nullification, November 24, 1832.

www.docsouth.unc.edu—Out of print works of southern nonfiction including *Emma LeConte's Diary.*

PERSONAL INTERVIEWS:
Lester Bates, Jr., January 2003, memories of Lester Bates, Sr.

Miriam Ford, August 2002, memories of Columbia people, Joe Berry, and Berry's On Main.

Katherine Keyes, February 2003, family oral history and geneology of Reverend Henry Mood.

Margaret Autry Sims, 2001–2003.

158

INDEX

The African American History Monument was dedicated on March 26, 2001. It was the first in the United States to be erected on state capitol grounds. The 23-foot granite obelisk is the centerpiece of two curved granite walls depicting scenes of African American history. (Photo by Burke Salsi.)